EAST INDIA
Publishing Company

OLIVER CROMWELL
Theodore Roosevelt

Published by the
EAST INDIA PUBLISHING COMPANY
Ottawa, Canada

Cover Design by EIPC © 2022
9781774266779

www.eastindiapublishing.com

CONTENTS

I. THE TIMES AND THE MAN

For over a century and a half after his death the memory of the greatest Englishman of the seventeenth century was looked upon with horror by the leaders of English thought, political and literary; the very men who were carrying to fruition Cromwell's tremendous policies being often utterly ignorant that they were following in his footsteps. At last the scales began to drop from the most far-seeing eyes. Macaulay, with his eminently sane and wholesome spirit, held Cromwell and the social forces for which he stood—Puritanic and otherwise—at their real worth, and his judgment about them was, in all essentials, accurate. But the true appreciation of the place held by the greatest soldier-statesman of the seventeenth century began with the publication of his life and letters by Carlyle. The gnarled genius of the man who worshipped the heroes of the past as intensely as he feared and distrusted the heroes of the present, enabled him to write with a loftiness and intensity that befitted his subject. But Carlyle's singular incapacity to "see veracity," as he would himself have phrased it, made him at times not merely tell half-truths, but deliberately invert the truth. He was of that not uncommon cloistered type which shrinks shuddering from actual contact with whatever it, in theory, most admires, and which, therefore, is reduced in self-justification to misjudge and misrepresent those facts of past history which form precedents for what is going on before the author's own eyes.

Cromwell lived in an age when it was not possible to realize a government based upon those large principles of social, political, and religious liberty in which—at any rate, during his earlier years—he sincerely believed; but the movement of which he was the head was the first of the great movements which, marching along essentially the same lines, have produced the English-speaking world as we at present know it. This primary fact Carlyle refused to see, or at least to admit. As the central idea of his work he states that the Puritanism of the Cromwellian epoch was the "last glimpse of the Godlike vanishing from this England; conviction and veracity giving place to hollow cant and formulism.... The last of all our Heroisms.... We have wandered far away from the ideas which guided us in that century, and indeed which had guided us in all preceding centuries, but of which that century was the ultimate manifestation; we have wandered very far; and must endeavor to return and connect ourselves therewith again.... I will advise my reader to forget the modern methods of reform; not to remember that he has ever heard of a modern individual called by the name of 'Reformer,' if he would understand what the old meaning of the word was. The Cromwells, Pyms, and Hampdens, who were understood on the Royalist side to be fire-brands of the devil, have had still worse measure from the Dry-as-Dust philosophies and sceptical histories of later times. They really did resemble fire-brands of the devil if you looked at them through spectacles of a certain color, for fire is always fire; but by no spectacles, only by mere blindness and wooden-eyed spectacles, can the flame-girt heaven's messenger pass for a poor, mouldy Pedant and Constitution-monger such as these would make him out to be."

This is good writing of its kind; but the thought is mere "hollow cant and unveracity;" not only far from the truth, but the direct reverse of the truth. It is itself the wail of the pedant who does not know that the flame-girt heaven's messenger of truth is always a mere mortal to those who see him with the actual eyes of the flesh, although mayhap a great mortal; while to the closet philosopher his quality of flame-girtedness is rarely visible until a century or thereabouts has elapsed.

So far from this great movement, of which Puritanism was merely one manifestation, being the last of a succession of similar heroisms, it had practically very much less connection with what went before than with all that has guided us in our history since. Of course, it is impossible to draw a line with mathematical exactness between the different stages of history, but it is both possible and necessary to draw it with rough efficiency; and, speaking roughly, the epoch of the Puritans was the beginning of the great modern epoch of the English-speaking world—infinitely its greatest epoch. We have not "wandered far from the ideas that guided" the wisest and most earnest leaders in the century that saw Cromwell; on the contrary, these ideas were themselves very far indeed from those which had guided the English people in previous ages, and the ideas that now guide us represent on the whole what was best and truest in the thought of the Puritans. As for Pym and Hampden, their type had practically no representative in England prior to their time, while all the great legislative reformers since then have been their followers. The Hampden type—the purest and noblest of types—reached its highest expression in Washington. Pym, the man of great powers and great services, with a tendency to believe that Parliamentary government was the cure for all evils, followed to a line "the modern methods of reform," and was exactly the man who, if he had lived in Carlyle's day, Carlyle would have sneered at as a "constitution-monger." It was men of the kind of Hampden and Pym who, before Carlyle's own eyes, were striving in the British Parliament for the reforms which were to carry one stage farther the work of Hampden and Pym; who were endeavoring to secure for all creeds full tolerance; to give the people an ever-increasing share in ruling their own destinies; to better the conditions of social and political life. In the great American Civil War the master spirits in the contest for union and freedom were actuated by a fervor as intense as, and even finer than, that which actuated the men of the Long Parliament; while in rigid morality and grim devotion to what he conceived to be God's bidding, the Southern soldier, Stonewall Jackson, was as true a type of the "General of the Lord, with his Bible and his Sword," as Cromwell or Ireton.

The whole history of the movement which resulted in the establishment of the Commonwealth of England will be misread and misunderstood if we fail to appreciate that it was the first modern, and not the last mediæval, movement; if we fail to understand that the men who figured in it and the principles for which they contended, are strictly akin to the men and the principles that have appeared in all similar great movements since: in the English Revolution of 1688; in the American Revolution of 1776; and the American Civil War of 1861. We must keep ever in mind the essentially modern character of the movement if we are to appreciate its true inwardness, its true significance. Fundamentally, it was the first struggle for religious, political, and social freedom, as we now understand the terms. As was inevitable in such a first struggle, there remained even among the forces of reform much of what properly belonged to previous generations. In addition to the modern side there was a mediæval side, too. Just so far as this mediæval element obtained, the movement failed. All that there was of good and of permanence in it was due to the new elements.

To understand the play of the forces which produced Cromwell and gave him his chance, we must briefly look at the England into which he was born.

He saw the light at the close of the reign of Queen Elizabeth, in the last years of the Tudor dynasty, and he grew to manhood during the inglorious reign of the first English king of the inglorious House of Stuart. The struggle between the reformed churches and the ancient church, against which they were in revolt, was still the leading factor in shaping European politics, though other factors were fast assuming an equal weight. The course of the Reformation in England had been widely different from that which it had followed in other European countries. The followers of Luther and Calvin, whatever their shortcomings—and they were many and grievous—had been influenced by a fiery zeal for righteousness, a fierce detestation of spiritual corruption; but in England the Reformation had been undertaken for widely different reasons by Henry VIII. and his creatures, though the bulk of their followers were as sincere as their brethren on the Continent. Henry's purpose had been simple, namely, to transfer to himself the power and revenues of the Papacy, so far as he could seize them, and thus to add to the spiritual supremacy against which the leaders of the Reformation had revolted: the absolute sovereignty which the Tudors were seeking to establish in England. Elizabeth stood infinitely above her father in most respects; but in religious views they were not far apart, and in theory they were both believers in absolutism. They had no standing army, and they were always in want of money, so that in practice they never ventured seriously to offend the influential and moneyed classes. But under Henry the misery and suffering of the lower classes became very great, and the yeomen were largely driven from their lands, while much of Elizabeth's own administration consisted of efforts to grapple with the vagrancy and wretchedness which had been caused by the degradation of those who stood lowest in the social scale.

When the Stuarts took possession of the throne of England they found a people which, unlike the peoples of most of the neighboring States, had not fought out its religious convictions. The Reformation had deeply stirred men's souls. Religion had become a matter of vital and terrible importance to Protestant and to Catholic. Among the extremists, the men who had given the tone to the Reformation in Germany, Switzerland, Holland, and Scotland, religion, as they understood it, entered into every act of their lives. In England there were men of this stamp; but in the English Reformation they had played a wholly subordinate part; and indeed had been in almost as great danger as the Catholics. Their force, therefore, had not spent itself. It had been conserved, in spite of their desires.

Thus it happened that the high tide of extreme Protestantism was reached in England, not as in other Protestant countries, in the sixteenth century, but in the seventeenth. The Stuarts were the only Protestant kings who were not in religious sympathy with their Protestant subjects. In theory the Anglican Church of Henry and Elizabeth stood for what we would now regard as tyranny. What Henry VIII. strove to do with the Anglican Church is what has actually been done by the Czars with the Orthodox Church in Russia; but that which was possible with the eastern Slavs was not possible with the westernmost and freest of the Teutonic peoples. Yet in the actual event it was probably fortunate that the English Reformation took the shape it did; for under such conditions it was not marked by the intense fanaticism of the reformers elsewhere.

The Stuarts not only found themselves masters of a kingdom where, supposedly, they were spiritually supreme, while actually their claim to supremacy was certain to be challenged; they also found themselves at the head of a form of government which was to all appearances despotic, while the people over whom they bore sway, though slow to object to the forms, were extremely intolerant of the practices of despotism. The Tudors were unarmed despots, who disliked the old feudal nobility, and who found it for their interest to cultivate the commercial classes, and to form a new nobility of their own, based upon wealth. The men at the lowest round of the social ladder—the workingmen and farm laborers—were yet, as they remained for a couple of centuries, so unfit for the work of political combination that they could be safely disregarded by the masters of England. At times their discontent was manifested, generally in the shape of abortive peasant insurrections; but there was never need to consider them as of serious and permanent importance. The middle classes, however, had become very powerful, and to their material interests the Tudors always took care to defer. At the very close of her reign, Elizabeth, who was at heart as thorough a tyrant as ever lived, but who possessed that shrewd good sense which, if not the noblest, is perhaps on the whole the most useful of qualities in the actual workaday world, found herself face to face with her people on the question of monopolies; and as soon as she understood that they were resolutely opposed to her policy, she instantly yielded. In other words, the Tudor despotism was conditioned upon the despot's doing nothing of which the influential classes of the nation—the upper and middle classes—seriously disapproved; and this the Stuart kings could never understand.

Moreover, apart from the fact that the Stuarts were so much less shrewd and less able than the Tudors, there was the further fact that Englishmen as a whole were gradually growing more intolerant, not only of the practice but of the pretence of tyranny, whether in things material or in things spiritual. There was a moral awakening which rendered it impossible for Englishmen of the seventeenth century to submit to the brutal wrong-doing which marked the political and ecclesiastical tyranny of the previous century. The career of Henry VIII. could not have been paralleled in any shape when once England had begun to breed such men as went to the making of the Long Parliament.

Much of the aspiration after higher things took the form of spiritual unrest. It must always be remembered that the Protestant sects which established themselves in the northern half of Europe, although they warred in the name of religious liberty, had no more conception of it, as we of this day understand it, than their Catholic foes; and yet it must also be remembered that the bitter conflicts they waged prepared the way for the wide tolerance of individual difference in matters of religious belief which is among the greatest blessings of our modern life. An American Catholic and an American Protestant of to-day, whatever the difference between their theologies, yet in their ways of looking at real life, at its relation to religion, and the relations of religion and the State, are infinitely more akin to one another than either is to the men of his religious faith who lived three centuries ago. We now admit, as a matter of course, that any man may, in religious matters, profess to be guided by authority or by reason, as suits him best; but that he must not interfere with similar freedom of belief in others; and that all men, whatever their religious beliefs, have exactly the same political rights and are to be held to the same responsibility for the way they exercise these rights. Few indeed were the men who held such views at the time when Cromwell was growing to manhood. Holland was the State of all others in which there was the nearest approach to religious liberty; and even in Holland the bitterness of the Calvinists toward the Arminians was something which we can now scarcely understand. Arminius was no more at home in Geneva than in Rome; and his followers were prescribed by the most religious people of England, and so far as might be were driven from the realm. Calvinists and Lutherans felt as little inclination as Catholics to allow liberty of conscience to others; and as grotesque a compromise as ever was made in matters religious was that made in Germany, when it was decided that the peoples of the various German principalities should in mass accept the faiths of their respective princes.

Yet though the Reformers thus strove to establish for their own use the very religious intolerance against which they had revolted, the mere fact of their existence nullified their efforts. Sooner or later people who had exercised their own judgment, and had fought for the right to exercise it, were sure grudgingly to admit the same right in others. That time was as yet far distant. In Cromwell's youth all the leading Christian churches were fiercely intolerant. Unless we keep in mind that this was the general attitude, an attitude which necessarily affected even the greatest men, we cannot do justice to the political and social leaders of that age when we find them, as we so often do, adopting toward their religious foes policies from which we, of a happier age, turn with horror.

In England hatred of Roman Catholicism had become almost interchangeable with hatred of Spain. Spain had been the one dangerous foe which England had encountered under the Tudor dynasty, and the only war she had ever waged into which the religious element entered was the war which put upon the English roll of honor the names of her great sixteenth-century seamen, Drake and Hawkins, Howard and Frobisher. Throughout the sixteenth century Spain had towered above every other power of Europe in warlike might; and though the Dutch and English sailors had broken the spell of her invincibility at sea, on shore her soldiers retained their reputation for superior prowess, in spite of the victories of Maurice of Orange, until Gustavus Adolphus marched his wonderful army down from the frozen North. During Cromwell's youth and early manhood Spain was still the most powerful and most dreaded of European nations. Her government had become a mere tyranny; her religion fanatical bigotry of a type more extreme than any that existed elsewhere, even in an age when all creeds tended toward fanaticism and bigotry. It was in Spain that the Holy Inquisition chiefly flourished—one of the most fearful engines for the destruction of all that was highest in mankind that the world has ever seen. Catholics were oppressed in England and Protestants in France; but in each country the persecuted sect might almost be said to enjoy liberty, and certainly to enjoy peace, when their fate was compared with the dreadful horrors of torture and murder with which Spain crushed out every species of heresy within her borders. Jew, Infidel, and Protestant, shared the same awful doom, until she had purchased complete religious uniformity at the price of the loss of everything that makes national life great and noble. The dominion of Spain would have been the dominion of desolation; her supremacy as baneful as that of the Turk; and Holland and England, in withstanding her, rendered the same service to humanity that was rendered at that very time by those nations of southeastern Europe who formed out of the bodies of their citizens the bulwark which stayed the Turkish fury.

But if in her relations to one Catholic nation England appeared as the champion of religious liberty, of all that makes life worth having to the free men who live in free nations, yet in her relations to another Catholic people she herself played the rôle of merciless oppressor—religious, political, and social. Ireland, utterly foreign in speech and culture, had been ground into the dust by the crushing weight of England's overlordship. During centuries chaos had reigned in the island; the English intruders possessing sufficient power to prevent the development of any Celtic national life, but not to change it into a Norman or English national life. The English who settled and warred in Ireland felt and acted as the most barbarous white frontiersmen of the nineteenth century have acted toward the alien races with whom they have been brought in contact. There is no language in which to paint the hideous atrocities committed in the Irish wars of Elizabeth; and the worst must be credited to the highest English officials. In Ireland the antagonism was fundamentally racial; whether the sovereign of England were Catholic or Protestant made little difference in the burden of wrong which the Celt was forced to bear. The first of the so-called plantations by which the Celts were ousted in mass from great tracts of country to make room for English settlers, was undertaken under the Catholic Queen Mary, and the two counties thus created by the wholesale expulsion of the wretched kerne were named in honor of the Queen and of her spouse, the

Spanish Philip. Though Philip's bigotry made him the persecutor of heretics, it taught him no mercy toward those of his own faith but of a different nationality, whether Irish or Portuguese. When England became Protestant, Ireland stood steadfastly for the old faith; and religious was added to race hatred. In Spain the Holy Inquisition was the handmaid of grinding tyranny. In Ireland the Catholic priesthood was the sole friend, standby, and comforter of a hunted and despairing people. In the Netherlands and on the high seas Protestantism was the creed of liberty. In Ireland it was one of the masks worn by the alien oppressor.

France was Catholic, but her Catholicism differed essentially from that of Spain, and during the first part of the seventeenth century was quite as liberal as the Protestantism of England. When Cromwell was a child Henry of Navarre was on the French throne, and to him all creeds were alike. He was succeeded in the actual government of France by the great Cardinals Richelieu and Mazarin, who were Statesmen rather than Churchmen; and under them the French Protestants enjoyed rather more toleration than was allowed the Catholics of England. The natural foes of France were the two great Catholic powers of Spain and Austria, ruled by the twin branches of the House of Hapsburg; and her hostility to them determined her attitude throughout the Thirty Years' War.

Meanwhile, Holland was at the height of her power. She had a far greater colonial empire than England, her commercial development was greater, and the renown of her war marine higher. Drake and Hawkins had but singed the beard of the Spanish king, had but plundered his vessels and harassed his great fleets. Van Heemskirk, Piet Hein, and the elder Tromp crushed the sea-power of Spain by downright hard fighting in great pitched battles, and captured her silver fleets entire.

In Great Britain itself—it must be kept in mind that Scotland was as yet an entirely distinct kingdom, united to England only by the fact that the same line of kings ruled over both—the difference between the Scotch and the English, though less in degree, was the same in kind as that between the English and the Dutch. In Scotland, outside of the Highlands, the mass of the people were devoted with all the strength of their intense and virile natures to the form of Calvinism introduced by Knox. Their Church government was Presbyterian. As both the Presbyterian ministers and their congregations demanded that the State should be managed in essentials according to the wishes of the Church, the general feeling was really in the direction of a theocratic republic, although the name would have frightened them. In Scotland, as in England, no considerable body of men had yet grasped the idea that there should be toleration of religious differences or a divorce between the functions of the State and the Church. In both countries, as elsewhere at the time through Christendom, religious liberty meant only religious liberty for the sect that raised the cry; but, as elsewhere, the mere use of the name as a banner under which to fight brought nearer the day when the thing itself would be possible.

In England there was practically peace during the first forty years of the century, but it was an ignoble and therefore an evil peace. Of course, peace should be the aim of all statesmen, and is the aim of the greatest statesman. Nevertheless, not only the greatest statesmen, but all men who are truly wise and patriotic, recognize that peace is good only when it comes honorably and is used for honorable purposes, and that the peace of mere sloth or incapacity is as great a curse as the most unrighteous war. Those who doubt this would do well to study the condition of England during the reign of James I., and during the first part of the reign of Charles I. England had then no standing army and no foreign policy worthy of the name. The chief of her colonies was growing up almost against her wishes, and wholly without any help or care from her. In short, she realized the conditions, as regards her relations with the outside world and "militarism," which certain philosophers advocate at the present day for America. The result was a gradual rotting of the national fibre, which rendered it necessary for her to pass through the fiery ordeal of the Civil War in order that she might be saved.

In every nation there is, as there has been from time immemorial, a good deal of difficulty in combining the policies of upholding the national honor abroad, and of preserving a not too heavily taxed liberty at home. Many peoples and many rulers who have solved the problem with marked success as regards one of the two conditions, have failed as regards the other. It was the peculiar privilege of the Stuart kings to fail signally in both. They were dangerous to no one but their own subjects. Their government was an object of contempt to their neighbors and of contempt, mixed with anger and terror, to their own people. They made amends for utter weakness in the face of a foreign foe by showing against the free men of their own country that kind of tyranny which finds its favorite expression in oppressing those who resist not at all, or ineffectually. They were held on the throne only by a mistaken but honorable loyalty, and by an unworthy servility; by the strong habits formed by the customs of centuries; and, most of all, by the wise distrust of radical innovation and preference for reform to revolution which gives to the English race its greatest strength.

This last attitude, the dislike of revolution, was entirely wholesome and praiseworthy. On the other hand, the doctrine of the divine right of kings, which represented the extreme form of loyalty to the sovereign, was vicious, unworthy of the race, and to be ranked among degrading superstitions. It is now so dead that it is easy to laugh at it; but it was then a real power for evil. Moreover, the extreme zealots who represented the opposite pole of the political and religious world, were themselves, as is ordinarily the case with such extremists, the allies of the forces against which they pretended to fight. From these dreamers of dreams, of whose "cloistered virtue" Milton spoke with such fine contempt, the men who possessed the capacity to do things turned contemptuously away, seeking practical results rather than theoretical perfection, and being content to get the substance at some cost of form. As always, the men who counted were those who strove for actual achievement in the field of practical politics, and who were not misled merely by names. England, in the present century, has shown how complete may be the freedom of the individual under a nominal monarchy; and the Dreyfus incident in France would be proof enough, were any needed, that despotism of a peculiarly revolting type may grow rankly, even in a republic, if there is not in its citizens a firm and lofty purpose to do justice to all men and guard the rights of the weak as well as of the strong.

James came to the throne to rule over a people steadily growing to think more and more seriously of religion: to believe more and more in their rights and liberties. But the King himself was cursed with a fervent belief in despotism, and an utter inability to give his belief practical shape in deeds. For half a century the spirit of sturdy independence had been slowly growing among Englishmen. Elizabeth governed almost under the forms of despotism; but a despotism which does not carry the sword has to accommodate itself pretty thoroughly to the desires of the subjects, once these desires become clearly defined and formulated. Elizabeth never ventured to do what Henry had done. She left England, therefore, thoroughly Royalist, devoted to the Crown, and unable to conceive of any other form of government, but already desirous of seeing an increase in the power of the people as expressed through Parliament. James, from the very outset of his reign, pursued a course of conduct exactly fitted both to irritate the people, with the pretensions of the Crown, and to convince them that they could prevent these pretensions from being carried out.

Besides, he offended both their political and their religious feelings. England had been growing more and more fanatically Protestant; that is, more and more Puritan. Under Elizabeth there had been more religious persecution of Puritans, and of Dissenters generally, than of Catholics. But this could not prevent the growth of the spirit of Puritanism. During the reign of James there were marked Presbyterian tendencies visible within the Anglican Church itself, and plenty of Puritans among her divines. Unfortunately, both Presbyterian and Anglican were then at one in heartily condemning that spirit of true religious liberty, of true toleration, which we of to-day in the United States recognize as the most vital of religious rights. The so-called Independent movement, from which sprang the Congregational and indeed the Baptist Churches as we know them to-day, had begun under Elizabeth. Its votaries contended for what now seems the self-evident right of each congregation, if it so desires, to decide for itself important questions of doctrine and of church management. Yet Elizabeth's ministers had actually stamped this sect out of existence, with the hearty approval of the wisest men in the realm and of the enormous majority of the people. Such an act, and, above all, such approval, shows how long and difficult was the road which still had to be traversed before the goal of religious liberty was reached.

The people were relatively less advanced toward religious than toward political liberty. Nevertheless, they were distinctly in advance of the King, even in matters religious. The resolute determination to fight for one's own liberty of conscience, when it once becomes the characteristic of the majority, cannot but tend toward securing liberty of conscience for all; whereas, for one man, who claims supremacy in the Church as well as overlordship in the State, to seek to impose his will upon others in matters both spiritual and political, cannot but produce a very aggravated form of tyranny. The Stuarts represented an extreme, reactionary type of kingship; a type absolutely alien to all that was highest and most characteristic in the English character. They possessed the will to be despots, but neither their own powers nor the tendencies of the times were in their favor. The tendency was, however, very strongly in favor of hereditary kingship; so strongly, indeed, that nothing but the extreme folly as well as the extreme baseness of the Stuart kings could overcome it. Stability of government, and therefore order, depends in the last resort upon the ability of the people to come to a consensus as to where power belongs. This consensus is less a matter of volition than of long habit, of slow evolution; to Americans of to-day, the rule of the majority seems part of the natural order of things, whereas to Russians it seems utterly unnatural, and they could by no possibility be brought into sudden acquiescence in it. To Englishmen, in the early decades of the seventeenth century, hereditary kingship seemed the only natural government, and they could be severed from this belief only by a succession of violent wrenches.

James I. stood for absolutism in Church and State, and quarrelled with and annoyed his subjects in the futile effort to realize his ideas. Charles I., whom James had vainly sought to marry to a Spanish princess, and succeeded in marrying to a French princess (Henrietta Maria), took up his father's task. In private life he was the best of the Stuart kings, reaching about the average level of his subjects. In public life his treachery, mendacity, folly, and vindictiveness: his utter inability to learn by experience or to sympathize with any noble ambition of his country: his readiness to follow evil counsel, and his ingratitude toward any sincere friend, made him as unfit as either of his sons to sit on the English throne; and a greater condemnation than this it is not possible to award. Germany was convulsed by the Thirty Years' War: but Charles cared nothing for the struggle, and to her humiliation England had to see Sweden step to the front as the champion of the Reformation. At one period Charles even started to help the French king against the Huguenots, but was brought to a halt by the outburst of wrath this called forth from his subjects. Once he made feeble war on Spain, and again he made feeble war on France; but the expedition he sent against Cadiz failed, and the expedition he sent to Rochelle was beaten; and he was, in each case, forced to make peace without gaining anything. The renown of the English arms never stood lower than during the reigns of the first two Stuarts.

At the outset of his reign Charles sought to govern through Buckingham, who was entirely fit to be his minister, and, therefore, unfit to be trusted with the slightest governmental task on behalf of a free and great people. Under Buckingham the grossest corruption obtained—not only in the public service, but in the creation of peerages. His whole administration represented nothing but violence and bribery; and when he took command of the forces to be employed against Rochelle, he showed that the list of his qualities included complete military incapacity.

It was after the failure at Rochelle that Charles summoned his third Parliament. With his first two he had failed to do more than quarrel, as they would not grant him supplies unless they were allowed the right to have something to say as to how they were to be used. He had, therefore, dissolved them, holding that their only function was to give him what may be needed.

With his third Parliament he got on no better. In it two great men sprang to the front—Sir Thomas Wentworth, afterward Lord Strafford, and Sir John Eliot, who had already shown himself a leader of the party that stood for free representative institutions as against the unbridled power of the King. Eliot was a man of pure and high character, and of dauntless resolution, though a good deal of a doctrinaire in his belief that Parliamentary government was the cure for all the evils of the body politic. Wentworth, dark, able, imperious, unscrupulous, was a born leader, but he had no root of true principle in him. At the moment, from jealousy of Buckingham, and from desire to show that he would have to be placated if the King were awake to self-interest, he threw all the weight of his great power on the popular side.

Instead of giving the King the money he wanted, Parliament formulated a Petition of Right, demanding such elementary measures of justice as that the King should agree never again to raise a forced loan, or give his soldiers free quarters on householders, or execute martial law in time of peace, or send whom he wished to prison without showing the cause for which it was done. The last was the provision against which Charles struggled hardest. The Star Chamber—a court which sat without a jury, and which was absolutely under the King's jurisdiction—had been one of his favorite instruments in working his arbitrary will. The powers of this court were left untouched by the Petition: yet even the service this court could render him was far less than what he could render himself if it lay in his power arbitrarily to imprison men without giving the cause. However, his need of money was so great, and the Commons stood so firm, that he had to yield, and on June 7th, in the year 1628, the Petition of Right became part of the law of the land. The first step had been taken toward cutting out of the English Constitution the despotic powers which the Tudor kings had bequeathed to their Stuart successors.

Immediately afterward Buckingham was assassinated by a

soldier who had taken a violent grudge against him, and the nation breathed freer with this particular stumbling-block removed, while it lessened the strain between the King and the Commons, who were bent on his impeachment.

There were far more serious troubles ahead. If the King could raise money without summoning Parliament, he could rule absolutely. If Parliament could control not only the raising, but the expenditure of money, it would be the supreme source of power, and the King but a figure-head; in other words, the government would be put upon the basis on which it has actually stood during the present century. For many reigns the Commons had been accustomed to vote to each king for life, at the outset of his reign, the duties on exports and imports, known as tonnage and poundage; but during the years immediately past men had been forced to think much on liberty and self-government. Parliament was in no mood to surrender absolute power to the King.

With the right to lay taxes and to supervise the expenditure of money—that is, to conduct the government—was intertwined the question of religion. The mass of Englishmen adhered rather loosely to the Anglican communion, and were not extreme Puritans; on certain points, however, they were tinged very deeply with Calvinism. They were greatly angered by the attitude of those bishops, who under the lead of Laud showed themselves more hostile to Protestant than to Catholic dogmas. These bishops preached not only that the views in Church matters held by the bulk of Englishmen were wrong, but furthermore that it was the duty of every subject to render entire obedience to the sovereign, no matter what the sovereign did, and they insisted that parliaments were of right mere ciphers in the State. Such doctrines were not only irritating from the theological stand-point; they also struck at the root of political freedom. The religious antagonism was accentuated by the fact that at this time the Protestant cause in Germany had touched the lowest point it ever reached during the Thirty Years' War, and the anger and alarm of the English Protestants, as they saw the Calvinists and Lutherans of Denmark and North Germany overcome, were heightened by the indifference, if not satisfaction, with which the King and the bishops looked at the struggle.

In 1629 the Commons, under the lead of Eliot and Pym, took advanced ground alike on the questions of religion and of taxation. Pym was supplementing Eliot's work, which was to make the House of Commons the supreme authority in England, by striving to associate together a majority of the members for the achievement of certain common objects; in other words, he was laying the foundation of party government. Under the lead of these two men, the first two Parliamentary and popular leaders in the modern sense, the House of Commons passed resolutions demanding uniformity in religious belief throughout the kingdom and condemning every innovation in religion, and declaring enemies to the kingdom and traitors to its liberties whoever advised the levying of tonnage and poundage without the authority of Parliament, or whoever voluntarily paid those duties. The first clause hit Catholics and Dissenters alike, but was especially aimed at the bishops and their followers, who stood closest to the King; and the second was, of course, intended to transfer the sovereignty from the King to Parliament—in other words, from the King to the people. Charles met the challenge by dissolving Parliament. Eleven years were to pass before another met. Meantime, the King governed as a despot; and it must be remembered that when he deliberately chose thus to govern as a despot, responsible to no legal tribunal, he at once threw his subjects back on the only remedies which it is possible to enforce against despotism—deposition or death.

Charles was bitterly angry at the sturdy independence shown by the Commons, and marked out for vengeance those who had been foremost in thwarting his wishes. His course was easy. The Petition of Right formulated a principle, but as yet it offered no safeguard against an unscrupulous king; while the Star Chamber court, and the other judges for that matter, held office at his pleasure, and acted as his subservient tools in fining and imprisoning merchants who refused payment of the duties, or men whose acts or words the king chose to consider seditious. Eliot and some of his fellow-members were thrown into prison because of the culminating proceedings in Parliament. Eliot's comrades made submission and were released, but Eliot refused to acknowledge that the King, through his courts, had any right to meddle with what was done in Parliament. He took his stand firmly on the ground that the King was not the master of Parliament, and of course this could but mean ultimately that Parliament was master of the King. In other words, he was one of the earliest leaders of the movement which has produced English freedom and English government as we now know them. He was also its martyr. He was kept in the Tower without air or exercise for three years, the King vindictively refusing to allow the slightest relaxation in his confinement, even when it brought on consumption. In December, 1632, he died; and the King's hatred found its last expression in denying to his kinsfolk the privilege of burying him in his Cornish home.

Charles set eagerly to work to rule the kingdom by himself. To the Puritan dogma of enforced unity of religious belief—utterly mischievous, and just as much fraught with slavery to the soul in one sect as another—he sought, through Laud, to oppose the only less mischievous, because silly, doctrine of enforced uniformity in the externals of public worship. Laud was a small and narrow man, hating Puritanism in every form, and persecuting bitterly every clergyman or layman who deviated in any way from what he regarded as proper ecclesiastical custom. His tyranny was of that fussy kind which, without striking terror, often irritates nearly to madness. He was Charles's instrument in the effort to secure ecclesiastical absolutism.

The instrument through which the King sought to establish the royal prerogative in political affairs was of far more formidable temper. Immediately after the dissolution of Parliament Wentworth had obtained his price from the King, and was appointed to be his right-hand man in administering the kingdom. A man of great shrewdness and insight, he seems to have struggled to govern well, according to his lights; but he despised law and acted upon the belief that the people should be slaves, unpermitted, as they were unfit, to take any share in governing themselves. After a while Laud was made archbishop; and Wentworth was later made Lord Strafford.

Wentworth and Laud, with their associates, when they tried to govern on such terms, were continually clashing with the people. A government thus carried on naturally aroused resistance, which often itself took unjustifiable forms; and this resistance was, in its turn, punished with revolting brutality. Criticism of Laudian methods, or of existing social habits, might take scurrilous shape; and then the critic's ears were hacked off as he stood in the pillory, or he was imprisoned for life.

The great fight was made, not on a religious, but on a purely political question—that of Ship Money. The king wished to go to war with the Dutch, and to raise his fleet he issued writs, first to the maritime counties, and then to every shire in England. He consulted his judges, who stated that his action was legal: as well they might, for when a judge disagreed with him on any important point, he was promptly dismissed from office. But there was one man in the kingdom who thought differently, John Hampden, a Buckinghamshire 'squire, who had already once sat as a silent member in Parliament, together with another equally silent member of the same social standing, his nephew, Oliver Cromwell. Hampden was assessed at twenty shillings. The amount was of no more importance than the value of the tea which a century and a half later was thrown into Boston Harbor; but in each case a vital principle—the same vital principle—was involved. If the King could take twenty shillings from Hampden without authority from the representatives of the people in Parliament assembled, then his rule was absolute: he could do what he pleased. On the other hand, if the House of Commons could do as it wished in granting money only for whatever need it chose to recognize in the kingdom, then the House of Commons was supreme. In Hampden's view but one course was possible—he was for the Parliament and the nation against the King; and he refused to pay the sum, facing without a murmur the punishment for his contumacy.

The King and his ministers did not flinch from proceeding to any length against either political or religious opponents. Charles heartily upheld Laud and Wentworth in carrying out their policy of "thorough"; Laud in England; Wentworth, after 1633, in Ireland. "Thorough," in their sense of the word, meant making the State, which was the King, paramount in every ecclesiastical and political matter, and putting his interests above the interests, the principles, and the prejudices of all classes and all parties; paying heed to nothing but to what seemed right in the eyes of the sovereign and the sovereign's chosen advisers. Under Wentworth's strong hand a certain amount of material prosperity followed in Ireland, although chiefly among the English settlers. There was no such material prosperity in England; 1630, for instance, was a famine year. The net effect of the policy would in the long run have been to bring down a freedom-loving people to a lower grade of political and social development. There was, of course, no oppression in England in any way resembling such oppression as that which flogged the Dutch to revolt against the Spaniards. But it was exactly the kind of oppression which led, in 1776, to the American Revolution. Eliot, Hampden, and Pym, stood for the principles that were championed by Washington, Patrick Henry, and the Adamses. The grievances which forced the Long Parliament to appeal to arms were like those which made the Continental Congress throw off the sovereignty of George III. In neither case was there the kind of grinding tyranny which has led to the assassination of tyrants and the frantic, bloodthirsty uprising of tortured slaves. In each case the tyranny was in its first stage, not its last; but the reason for this was simply that a nation of vigorous freemen will always revolt by the time the first stage has been reached. It was not possible, either for the Stuart kings or for George III., to go beyond a certain point, for as soon as that point was reached the freemen were called to arms by their leaders.

However, there was the greatest reluctance among Englishmen to countenance rebellion, even for the best of causes. This reluctance was eminently justifiable. Rebellion, revolution—the appeal to arms to redress grievances; these are measures that can only be justified in extreme cases. It is far better to suffer any moderate evil, or even a very serious evil, so long as there is a chance of its peaceable redress, than to plunge the country into civil war; and the men who head or instigate armed rebellions for which there is not the most ample justification must be held as one degree worse than any but the most evil tyrants. Between the Scylla of despotism and the Charybdis of anarchy there is but little to choose; and the pilot who throws the ship upon one is as blameworthy as he who throws it on the other. But a point may be reached where the people have to assert their rights, be the peril what it may; and in Great Britain this point was passed under Charles I.

The first break came, not in England, but in Scotland. The Scotch abhorred Episcopacy; whereas the English had no objection whatever to bishops, so long as the bishops did not outrage the popular religious convictions. In Scotland the spirit of Puritanism was uppermost, and was already exhibiting both its strength and its weakness; its sincerity and its lack of breadth; its stern morality and its failure to discriminate between essentials and non-essentials; its loftiness of aim and its tendency to condemn liberality of thought in religion, art, literature, and science, alike as irreligious; its insistence on purity of life, and yet its unconscious tendency to promote hypocrisy and to drive out one form of religious tyranny merely to erect another.

A man of any insight would not have striven to force an alien system of ecclesiastical government upon a people so stubborn and self-reliant, who were wedded to their own system of religious thought. But this was what Laud attempted, with the full approval of Charles. In 1637 he made a last effort to introduce the ceremonies of the English Church at Edinburgh. No sooner was the reading of the Prayer-Book begun than the congregation burst into wild uproar, execrating it as no better than celebrating mass. It was essentially a popular revolt. The incident of Jenny Geddes's stool may be mythical, but it was among the women and men of the lower orders that the resistance was stoutest. The whole nation responded to the cry, and hurried to sign a national Covenant, engaging to defend the Reformed religion, and to do away with all "innovations"; that is, with everything in which Episcopacy differed from Puritanism and inclined toward the Church of Rome.

In England and Scotland alike the Church of Rome was still accepted by the people at large as the most dangerous of enemies. The wonderful career of Gustavus Adolphus had just closed. The Thirty Years' War—the last great religious struggle—was still at its height. If, in France, the Massacre of St. Bartholomew stood far in the past, the Revocation of the Edict of Nantes yet lay in the future. The after-glow of the fires of Smithfield still gleamed with lurid light in each sombre Puritan heart. The men who, in England, were most earnest about their religion held to their Calvinistic creed with the utmost sincerity, high purpose, and self-devotion: but with no little harshness. Theirs was a lofty creed, but one which, in the revolt against levity and viciousness, set up a standard of gloom; and, though ready to fight to the death for liberty for themselves, they had as yet little idea of tolerating liberty in others. Naturally, such men sympathized with one another, and the action of the Scotch was heartily, though secretly, applauded by the stoutest Presbyterians of England. Moreover, while menaced by the common oppressor, the Puritan independents, who afterward split off from the Presbyterians, made common cause with them, the irreconcilable differences between the two bodies not yet being evident.

Soon the Scotch held a general assembly of the Church, composed of both clerical and lay members, and formally abolished Episcopacy, in spite of the angry protests of the King. Their action amounted in effect to establishing a theocracy. They repudiated the unlimited power of the King and the bishops, as men would do nowadays in like case; but they declared against liberty of thought and conduct in religious matters, basing their action on practically the same line of reasoning that influenced the very men they most denounced, hated, and feared.

The King took up the glove which the Scotch had thrown down. He raised an army and undertook the first of what were derisively known as the "Bishops' Wars." But his people sympathized with the Scotch rather than with him. He got an army together on the Border, but it would not fight, and he was forced reluctantly to treat for peace. Then Strafford came back from Ireland and requested Charles to summon a Parliament so that he could get funds. In April, 1640, the Short Parliament came together, but the English spirit was now almost as high as the Scotch in hostility to the King, and Parliament would not grant anything to the King until the grievances of the people were redressed. To this demand Charles would not listen, and the Parliament was promptly dissolved. Then, being heartened by Laud, and especially by Strafford, Charles renewed the war, only to see his army driven in headlong panic before the Scotch at Newburn. The result was that he had to try to patch up a peace under the direction of Strafford. But the Scotch would not leave the kingdom until they were paid the expenses of the war. There was no money to pay them, and Charles had to summon Parliament once more. On November 3d, 1640, the Long Parliament met at Westminster.

When Oliver Cromwell took his seat in the Long Parliament he was forty-one years old. He had been born at Huntingdon on April 25, 1599, and by birth belonged to the lesser gentry, or upper middle-class. The original name of the family had been Williams; it was of Welsh origin. There were many Cromwells, and Oliver was a common name among them. One of the Protector's uncles bore the name, and remained a stanch Loyalist throughout the Civil War. Oliver's own father, Robert, was a man in very moderate circumstances, his estate in the town of Huntingdon bringing an income of some £300 a year. Oliver's mother, Elizabeth Steward of Ely, seems to have been of much stronger character than his father. The Stewards, like the Cromwells, were "new people," both families, like so many others of the day, owing their rise to the spoliation of the monasteries. Oliver's father was a brewer, and his success in the management of the brewery was mainly due to Oliver's mother. No other member of Oliver's family—neither his wife nor his father—influenced him as did his mother. She was devoted to him, and he, in turn, loved her tenderly and respected her deeply. He followed her advice when young; he established her in the Royal Palace of Whitehall when he came to greatness; and when she died he buried her in Westminster Abbey. As a boy he received his education at Huntingdon, but when seventeen years old was sent to Cambridge University. A strong, hearty young fellow; fond of horse-play and rough pranks—as indeed he showed himself to be even when the weight of the whole kingdom rested on his shoulders. He nevertheless seems to have been a fair student, laying the foundation for that knowledge of Greek literature and the Latin language, and that fondness for books, which afterward struck the representatives of the foreign powers at London. In 1617 his father died, and he left Cambridge. When twenty-one years old he was married in London, to Elizabeth Bouchier (who was one year older than he was), the daughter of a rich London furrier. She was a woman of gentle and amiable character, and though she does not appear to have influenced Cromwell's public career to any perceptible extent, he always regarded her with fond affection, and was always faithful to her.

For twenty years after his marriage he lived a quiet life, busying himself with the management of his farm. Nine children were born to him, of whom three sons and five daughters lived to maturity. About this time his soul was first deeply turned toward religious matters, and, like the great majority of serious thinkers of the time, he became devoted to the Puritan theology; indeed no other was possible to a representative of the prosperous, independent, and religious middle-class, from which all the greatest Puritan leaders sprang. While a boy Oliver had been sent to the free school at Huntingdon, and his first training had been received under its master, the Reverend Thomas Beard, a zealous Puritan and Reformer, as well as a man of wide reading and sound scholarship, and lastly, an inflamed hater of the Church of Rome. All his surroundings, all his memories, were such as to make the future Dictator of England sincerely feel that the Church of Rome was the arch-antagonist of all, temporal and spiritual, that he held most dear. In the first place his ancestors were among those who had profited by the spoliation of the monasteries; and the only way to avoid uncomfortable feelings on the part of the spoiler is for him to show—or if this is not possible, to convince himself that he has shown—the utmost iniquity on the part of the despoiled. When Oliver was a small boy the Gunpowder Plot shook all England.

When he was a little older Henry of Navarre was stabbed in Paris; and though Henry was a cynical turncoat in matters of religion, and a man of the most revolting licentiousness in private life, he was yet a great ruler of men, and had been one of the props of the Protestant cause. Before Oliver came of age the Thirty Years' War had begun its course. To Oliver Cromwell, warfare against the Church of Rome, broken by truces which, whether long or short, were intended only to be breathing-spells, must have seemed the normal state of things.

In 1631 Oliver sold his paternal estate in Huntingdon and managed a rented farm at St. Ives for five years; then he removed to Ely, in the fen country, and again took up farming, being joined by his mother and sisters. He served in the great Parliament which passed the Petition of Right, but played no part of prominence therein: standing stoutly, however, for Puritanism and Parliamentary freedom. During the ensuing eleven years of unrest, while all England was making ready for the impending conflict, Oliver busied himself with his farm and his family. He showed himself one of the strongest bulwarks of the Puritan preachers; zealous in the endeavor to further the cause of religion in every way, and always open to appeals from the poor and the oppressed, of whom he was the consistent champion. When certain rich men, headed by the Earl of Bedford, endeavored to oust from some of their rights the poor people of the fens, Oliver headed the latter in their resistance. He was keenly interested in the trial of his kinsman, John Hampden, for refusal to pay the Ship Money; a trial which was managed by the advocate Oliver St. John, his cousin by marriage.

In short, Cromwell was far more concerned in righting specific cases of oppression than in advancing the great principles of constitutional government which alone make possible that orderly liberty which is the bar to such individual acts of wrong-doing. From the stand-point of the private man this is a distinctly better failing than is its opposite; but from the stand-point of the statesman the reverse is true. Cromwell, like many a so-called "practical" man, would have done better work had he followed a more clearly defined theory; for though the practical man is better than the mere theorist, he cannot do the highest work unless he is a theorist also. However, all Cromwell's close associations were with Hampden, St. John, and the other leaders in the movement for political freedom, and he acted at first in entire accord with their ideas: while with the religious side of their agitation he was in most hearty sympathy.

It is difficult for us nowadays to realize how natural it seemed at that time for the Word of the Lord to be quoted and appealed to on every occasion, no matter how trivial, in the lives of sincerely religious men. It is very possible that quite as large a proportion of people nowadays strive to shape their internal lives in accordance with the Ten Commandments and the Golden Rule; indeed, it is probable that the proportion is far greater; but professors of religion then carried their religion into all the externals of their lives. Cromwell belonged among those earnest souls who indulged in the very honorable dream of a world where civil government and social life alike should be based upon the Commandments set forth in the Bible. To endeavor to shape the whole course of individual existence in accordance with the hidden or half-indulged law of perfect righteousness, has to it a very lofty side; but if the endeavor is extended to include mankind at large, it has also a very dangerous side: so dangerous indeed that in practice the effort is apt to result in harm, unless it is undertaken in a spirit of the broadest charity and toleration; for the more sincere the men who make it, the more certain they are to treat, not only their own principles, but their own passions, prejudices, vanities, and jealousies, as representing the will, not of themselves, but of Heaven. The constant appeal to the Word of God in all trivial matters is, moreover, apt to breed hypocrisy of that sanctimonious kind which is peculiarly repellent, and which invariably invites reaction against all religious feeling and expression.

At that day Cromwell's position in this matter was, at its worst, merely that of the enormous majority of earnest men of all sects. Each sect believed that it was the special repository of the wisdom and virtue of the Most High: and the most zealous of its members believed it to be their duty to the Most High to make all other men worship Him according to what they conceived to be His wishes. This was the mediæval attitude, and represented the mediæval side in Puritanism; a side which was particularly prominent at the time, and which, so far as it existed, marred the splendor of Puritan achievement. The nobleness of the effort to bring about the reign of God on earth, the inspiration that such an effort was to those engaged in it, must be acknowledged by all; but, in practice, we must remember that, as religious obligation was then commonly construed, it inevitably led to the Inquisition in Spain; to the sack of Drogheda in Ireland; to the merciless persecution of heretics by each sect, according to its power, and the effort to stifle freedom of thought and stamp out freedom of action. It is right, and greatly to be desired, that men should come together to search after the truth: to try to find out the true will of God; but in Cromwell's time they were only beginning to see that each body of seekers must be left to work out its own beliefs without molestation, so long as it does not strive to interfere with the beliefs of others.

The great merit of Cromwell, and of the party of the Independents which he headed, and which represented what was best in Puritanism, consists in the fact that he and they did, dimly, but with ever-growing clearness, perceive this principle, and, with many haltings, strove to act up to it. The Independent or Congregational churches, which worked for political freedom, and held that each congregation of Protestants should decide for itself as to its religious doctrines, stood as the forerunners in the movement that has culminated in our modern political and religious liberty. How slow the acceptance of their ideas was, how the opposition to them battled on to the present century, will be appreciated by anyone who turns to the early writings of Gladstone when he was the "rising hope of those stern Tories," whose special antipathy he afterward became. Even yet there are advocates of religious intolerance, but they are mostly of the academic kind, and there is no chance for any political party of the least importance to try to put their doctrines into effect. More and more, at least here in the United States, Catholics and Protestants, Jews and Gentiles, are learning the grandest of all lessons—that they can best serve their God by serving their fellow-men, and best serve their fellow-men, not by wrangling among themselves, but by a generous rivalry in working for righteousness and against evil.

This knowledge then lay in the future. When Cromwell grew to manhood he was a Puritan of the best type, of the type of Hampden and Milton; sincere, earnest, resolute to do good as he saw it, more liberal than most of his fellow-religionists, and saved from their worst eccentricities by his hard common-sense, but not untouched by their gloom, and sharing something of their narrowness. Entering Parliament thus equipped, he could not fail to be most drawn to the religious side of the struggle. He soon made himself prominent; a harsh-featured, red-faced, powerfully-built man, whose dress appeared slovenly in the eyes of the courtiers—who was no orator, but whose great power soon began to impress friends and enemies alike.

II. THE LONG PARLIAMENT AND THE CIVIL WAR

King Charles's theory was that Parliament had met to grant him the money he needed. The Parliament's conviction was that it had come together to hold the King and his servants to accountability for what they had done, and to provide safeguards against a repetition of the tyranny of the last eleven years. Parliament held the whip hand, for the King dared not dissolve it until the Scots were paid, lest their army should march at once upon London.

The King had many courtiers who hated popular government, but he had only one great and terrible man of the type that can upbuild tyrannies; and, with the sure instinct of mortal fear and mortal hate, the Commons struck at the minister whose towering genius and unscrupulous fearlessness might have made his master absolute on the throne. A week after the Long Parliament met, in November, 1640, Pym, who at once took the lead in the House, moved the impeachment of Strafford, in a splendid speech which set forth the principles for which the popular party was contending. It was an appeal from the rule of irresponsible will to the rule of law, for the violation of which every man could be held accountable before some tribunal. About the same time Laud was thrown into the Tower; but at the moment there was no thought of taking his life, for the ecclesiastic was not—like the statesman—a mighty and fearsome figure, and though he had done as much evil as his feeble nature permitted, he had unquestionably been far more conscientious than the great Earl. Strafford had sinned against the light, for he had championed liberty until the King paid him his price and made him the most dangerous foe of his former friends. He now defended himself with haughty firmness, and the King strove in every way to help him. But the Commons passed a Bill of Attainder against him: and then Charles committed an act of fatal meanness and treachery. There was not one thing that Strafford had done, save by his sovereign's wish and in his sovereign's interest. By every consideration of honor and expediency Charles was bound to stand by him. But the Stuart King flinched. Deeming it for his own interest to let Strafford be sacrificed, he signed the death-warrant. "Put not your trust in Princes," said the fallen Earl when the news was brought to him, and he went to the scaffold undaunted.

Cromwell showed himself to be a man of mark in this Parliament; but he was not among the very foremost leaders. He had no great understanding of constitutional government, no full appreciation of the vital importance of the reign of law to the proper development of orderly liberty. His fervent religious ardor made all questions affecting faith and doctrine close to him; and his hatred of corruption and oppression inclined him to take the lead whenever any question arose of dealing, either with the wrongs done by Laud in the course of his religious persecutions, or with the irresponsible tyranny of the Star Chamber, and the sufferings of its victims. The bent of Cromwell's mind was thus shown right in the beginning of his parliamentary career. His desire was to remedy specific evils. He was too impatient to found the kind of legal and constitutional system which could alone prevent the recurrence of such evils. This tendency, thus early shown, explains, at least in part, why it was that later he deviated from the path trod by Hampden, and afterward by Washington and Washington's colleagues: showing himself unable to build up free government or to establish the reign of law, until he was finally driven to substitute his own personal government for the personal government of the King whom he had helped to dethrone, and put to death. Cromwell's extreme admirers treat his impatience of the delays and shortcomings of ordinary constitutional and legal proceedings as a sign of his greatness. It was just the reverse. In great crises it may be necessary to overturn constitutions and disregard statutes, just as it may be necessary to establish a vigilance committee, or take refuge in lynch law; but such a remedy is always dangerous, even when absolutely necessary; and the moment it becomes the habitual remedy, it is a proof that society is going backward. Of this retrogression the deeds of the strong man who sets himself above the law may be partly the cause and partly the consequence; but they are always the signs of decay.

The Commons had passed a law authorizing the election of a Parliament at least once in three years: which at once took away the King's power to attempt to rule without a Parliament; and in May they extorted from the King an act that they should not be dissolved without their own consent. Ship Money was declared to be illegal; the Star Chamber was abolished; and Tonnage and Poundage were declared illegal, unless levied by Act of Parliament. Then the Scotch army was paid off and returned across the Border. The best work of the Commons had now been done, and if they could have trusted the King it would have been well for them to dissolve; but the King could not be trusted, and, moreover, the religious question was pushed to the front. Laud's actions—actions taken with the full consent and by the advice of the King—had rendered the Episcopal form of Church government obnoxious. The House of Commons was Presbyterian, and it speedily became evident that it wished to establish the Presbyterian system of Church government in the place of Episcopacy; and, moreover, that it intended to be just as intolerant on behalf of Presbyterianism as the King and Laud had been on behalf of Episcopacy. There was a strong moderate party which the King might have rallied about him, but his incurable bad faith made it impossible to trust his protestations. He now made terms with the Scotch, in accordance with which they agreed not to interfere between himself and his English subjects in religious matters. He hoped thereby to deprive the Presbyterian English of their natural allies across the Border. This conduct, of itself, would have inflamed the increasing religious bitterness; but it was raised to madness by the news that came from Ireland at this time.

Inspired by the news of the revolt in Scotland and the troubles in England, the Irish had risen against their hereditary oppressors. It was the revolt of a race which rose to avenge wrongs as bitter as ever one people inflicted upon another; and it was inevitable that it should be accompanied by appalling outrages in certain places. It was on these outrages that the English fixed their eyes, naturally ignoring the generations of English evil-doing which had brought them about. A furious cry for revenge arose. Every Puritan, from Oliver Cromwell down, regarded the massacres as a fresh proof that Roman Catholics ought to be treated, not as professors of another Christian creed, but as cruel public enemies; and their burning desire for vengeance took the form, not merely of hostility to Roman Catholicism, but to the Episcopacy, which they regarded as in the last resort an ally of Catholicism.

In November, 1641, the Puritan majority in Parliament passed the Grand Remonstrance—which was a long indictment of Charles's conduct. Cromwell had now taken his place as among the foremost of the Root and Branch Party, who demanded the abolition of Episcopacy, and whose action drove all those who believed in the Episcopal form of Church government into the party of the King. He threw himself with eager vehemence into the Party of the Remonstrance, and after its bill was passed told Falkland that if it had been rejected by Parliament he would have sold all he had, and never again seen England.

For a moment the Puritan violence, which culminated in the Grand Remonstrance, provoked a reaction in favor of the King; but the King, by another act of violence, brought about a counter-reaction. In January, 1642, he entered the House of Commons, and in person ordered the seizure and imprisonment in the Tower of the five foremost leaders of the Puritan party, including Pym and Hampden. Such a course on his part could be treated only as an invitation to civil war. London, which before had been wavering, now rallied to the side of the Commons; the King left Whitehall; and it was evident to all men that the struggle between him and the Parliament had reached a point where it would have to be settled by the appeal to arms.

In August, 1642, King Charles planted the royal standard on the Castle of Nottingham, and the Civil War began. The Parliamentary forces were led by the Earl of Essex. They included some 20 regiments of infantry and 75 troops of horse, each 60 strong, raised and equipped by its own captain. Oliver Cromwell was captain of the Sixty-seventh Troop, and his kinsfolk and close friends were scattered through the cavalry and infantry. His sons served with or under him. One brother-in-law was quartermaster of his own troop; a second was captain of another troop. His future son-in-law, Henry Ireton, was captain of yet another; a cousin and a nephew were cornets. Another cousin, John Hampden, was colonel of a regiment of foot; so was Cromwell's close friend and neighbor, the after-time Earl of Manchester, who was much under his influence.

It was nearly a hundred years since England had been the scene of serious fighting, and Scotland had witnessed nothing more than brawls during that time. Elizabeth's war with Spain had been waged upon the ocean. However, thousands of English and Scotch adventurers had served in the Netherlands and in High Germany under the Dutch and Swedish generals. In both the Royal and Parliamentary armies there was a sprinkling of men—especially in the upper ranks of the officers—who had had practical experience of war on a large scale. The English people offered exceptionally fine material for soldiers; the population was still overwhelmingly rural and agricultural. In the cities the hardy mechanics and craftsmen were accustomed to sports in which physical prowess played a great part. The agricultural classes were far above the peasant serfs of Germany and France; and the gentry and yeomanry were accustomed to the use of the horse and the fowling-piece, and were devoted to field-sports. In courage, in hardihood, in intelligence, the level was high.

Although gunpowder had been in use for a couple of centuries, progress toward the modern arms of precision had been so slow that close-quarter weapons were still, on the whole, superior; and shock tactics rather than fire tactics were decisive. Artillery, though used on the field of battle, was never there a controlling factor, being of chief use in the assault of fortified places. The musketeers took so long to load their clumsy weapons that they could be used to best advantage only when protected, and they played a less important part on a pitched field than the great bodies of pikemen with which they were mingled. In England the cavalry had completely the upper hand of the infantry. It was used, not merely to finish the fight, but to smash unbroken and unshaken bodies of foot; and so great was its value in the open field that every effort was made by the commanders on both sides to keep it at the largest possible ratio to the whole army. Every decisive battle of the Civil War was made such by the cavalry. The arrangement of the armies was, invariably, with the infantry in the centre, the pikemen and the musketeers ordinarily alternating in clumps, while the cavalry was on both wings. The dragoons, though mounted, habitually fought on foot with their fire-pieces. Lancers were rarely used. The heavy cavalry were clad in cuirasses, and armed with long, straight swords and pistols. The light cavalry usually wore the buff coat, sometimes with a breast-piece, always with a helmet; and in addition to their sword and pistols, carried a carbine.

Throughout Europe, at this time, cavalry trusted altogether too much to their clumsy firearms, save when handled by some great natural leader of horse; and, in consequence, on the Continent, the infantry had won the upper hand. But it happened in the English Civil War that the only great leaders developed were cavalrymen; and so the horse retained throughout the mastery over the foot; although, as each arm was always pitted against the same arm in the opposing forces, the struggle frequently wore itself out before the victorious horse and victorious foot, if they belonged to different parties, could fight it out between them.

The Civil War opened with just such blundering and indecisive fighting as marked the opening of the American Civil War two centuries later. There was no hard and fast line, whether geographically or of caste, between the two parties; in every portion of England, and in every rank of society, there were to be found adherents both of the King and of the Commons; but, as a whole, the east and south of England were for the Parliament; the north and west were Royalist. The bulk of the aristocracy stood for the King; the bulk of the lesser gentry and yeomanry were against him. The revolutionary movement—as in America in 1776—received its main strength from the lesser gentry, small farmers, tradesmen, and upper-class mechanics and handicraftsmen. In America in 1776 there was no proletariat. So far as there was one in England in 1642, it took no interest in the struggle. The peasantry, the mass of the agricultural laborers, were inclined toward the King, though the men immediately above them in social position, who represented the lowest rank that had political influence, were the other way. The townsmen were generally for the Parliament.

In comparing the English Civil War of the seventeenth century with the American Civil War of the nineteenth, there are some curious points of similarity, no less than some very sharp contrasts. During the two centuries there had been a great growth in esteem for fixity of principle. In the English Civil War nothing was more common than for a man to change sides, and there was treachery even on the field of battle itself; whereas, in the American Civil War, though many of the leaders, like Lee and Thomas, were in great doubt as to the proper course to follow, yet when sides had once been taken, there was no flinching and no looking back. Moreover, there was far greater intensity of popular feeling in the American Civil War; even the States that were divided in opinion at the outset held no considerable mass of population which did not soon throw its weight on one side or the other; whereas, in the English Civil War there were large bodies of men who strove to avoid declaring for either side. At the very end of the contest, tens of thousands of persons, mainly peasants, organized under the title of Clubmen, with the avowed purpose of holding the scales even between the two sets of combatants, and of looking out for their own interests. The American Civil War was fought for the right of secession, and efforts were made—in Kentucky, for instance—to establish the right of a locality to be neutral. The "state rights" theory reached an almost equal development in some of the English counties during the Cromwellian contest. Yorkshire at one time declared for neutrality. The trained bands of Cornwall, when the Royalist forces were driven back within their borders, promptly turned out and drove off the pursuing Parliamentarians, but refused to obey orders to leave the county in pursuit of their foes, and disbanded to their own homes. Later, they repeated exactly the same course of procedure. There were at times local truces, or agreements as to the conditions of the contest in particular localities.

On both sides "associations" were formed, consisting of special groups of counties banded together intimately for the purposes of defence. The most important of these, the Eastern Association, included Cromwell's own home, taking in all of the middle East. This region was throughout the contest the backbone of resistance to the King. Its people were strongly Puritan in feeling, and it was they who gave Cromwell his strength: for they gave him his Ironsides; and furnished the famous New Model for the Parliamentary army which finished the war.

At the outset of the war many of the nobles raised regiments from among their own tenants, and the armies were of picturesque look, each regiment having its own uniform. The Guards of Lord Essex adopted the buff leather coat, which afterward became the uniform of the whole Roundhead army. Hampden's regiment was in green; the London trained bands in bright scarlet. Other regiments were clad in blue or gray. In the Cavalier army there were foot-guards in white and foot-guards in red; and among their horse, the Life Guards of the King—composed of lords and gentlemen who had no separate commands—wore plumed casques over their long curled locks, embroidered lace collars over their glittering cuirasses, gay scarfs, gilded sword-belts, and great-boots of soft leather doubled down below the knee.

The history of the English Civil War, like the history of the American Revolutionary War and the American Civil War, teaches two lessons. First, it shows that the average citizen of a civilized community requires months of training before he can be turned into a good soldier, and that raw levies—no matter how patriotic—are, under normal conditions, helpless before smaller armies of trained and veteran troops, and cannot strike a finishing blow even when pitted against troops of their own stamp. In the second place it teaches a lesson, which at first sight seems contradictory of the first, but is in reality not in the least so; namely, that there is nothing sacrosanct in the trade of the soldier. It is a trade which can be learned without special difficulty by any man who is brave and intelligent, who realizes the necessity of obedience, and who is already gifted with physical hardihood and is accustomed to the use of the horse and of weapons, to enduring fatigue and exposure, and to acting on his own responsibility, taking care of himself in the open.

Cromwell's troops were not regulars, like the professional soldiers of the Thirty Years' War; they were volunteers. After two or three years' service they became the finest troops that Europe could then show; just as by 1864 the volunteers of Grant and Lee had reached a grade of perfection which made them, for their own work, superior to any other of the armies then in existence.

Under modern conditions, in a great civilized state, the regular army is composed of officers who have as a rule been carefully trained to their work; who possess remarkably fine physique, and who are accustomed to the command of men and to taking the lead in emergencies; and the enlisted men have likewise been picked out with great care as to their bodily development; have been drilled until they handle themselves, their horses, and their weapons admirably, can cook for themselves, and are trained to the endurance of hardship and exposure under the conditions of march and battle. An ordinary volunteer or militia regiment from an ordinary civilized community, on the other hand, no matter how enthusiastic or patriotic, or how intelligent, is officered by lawyers, merchants, business men, or their sons, and contains in its ranks clerks, mechanics, or farmers' lads of varying physique, who have to be laboriously taught how to shoot and how to ride, and, above all, how to cook and to take care of themselves and make themselves comfortable in the open, especially when tired out by long marches, and when the weather is bad. At the outset such a regiment is, of course, utterly inferior to a veteran regular regiment, but after it has been in active service in the field for a year or two, so that its weak men have been weeded out, and its strong men have learned their duties—which can be learned far more rapidly in time of war than in time of peace—it becomes equal to any regiment. Moreover, if a regular regiment consists of raw recruits and is officered by men who have learned their profession only in the barracks and the study and on the parade ground, it may be a cause of very disagreeable surprise to those who have grown to regard the word "regular" as a kind of fetich.

Again, a volunteer regiment may have the wisdom to select officers for the highest positions who know how to handle men, who have seen actual soldiering, who possess natural capacity for leadership, eagerness to learn, and the good sense to know their own shortcomings; and the rank and file may be men of adventurous temper, already skilful riflemen, and of great bodily hardihood, accustomed to exposure, accustomed to cook—that is to say, to take care of their stomachs—to live in the open, to endure hardship and fatigue, and to take advantage of cover in battle. Such a regiment, especially if raised on the frontier, may, from the outset, prove itself equal to or better than any ordinary regular regiment—as has recently been shown by our troops in the Philippines, by the Australians and Canadians in South Africa, and, above all, by the Boers; and as was shown nearly a century ago by Hofer's Tyrolese and Andrew Jackson's backwoodsmen. Of course, no good traits will avail in the least if men are possessed with the belief that they cannot be taught anything, if they are not eager to obey and to learn; or if they do not possess a natural fighting edge.

So it is with the men in high command. The careful training in body and mind, and especially in character, gained in an academy like West Point, and the subsequent experience in the field, endow the regular officer with such advantages that, in any but a long war, he cannot be overtaken even by the best natural fighter. In the American Civil War, for instance, the greatest leaders were all West Pointers. Yet even there, by the end of the contest both armies had produced regimental, brigade, and division commanders, who though originally from civil life, had learned to know their business exactly as well as the best regular officers; and there was at least one such commander—Forrest—who, in his own class, was unequalled. If in a war the regular officers prove to have been trained merely to the pedantry of their profession, and do not happen to number men of exceptional ability in their ranks, then sooner or later the men who are born soldiers will come to the front, even though they have been civilians until late in life.

None of the men on the Parliamentary side who had received their training in the Continental armies amounted to much. On the Royalist side the only professional soldier who made his mark was Rupert; and Rupert, after a year or two, was decisively beaten by Cromwell—a great natural military genius, who, although a civilian till after forty, showed an astonishing aptitude in grasping the essentials of his new profession. His only military rival in the war was Montrose, who was also not a professional soldier.

In September King Charles had gathered a force of 10,000 men at Nottingham, while Essex was getting together a larger army not far off, at Northampton. The wealth of the kingdom was with the Parliament, which also possessed the arsenal, the fleet, and the principal ports. On the other hand, man for man, the King's troops were superior to the Parliament's, especially in the most dreaded arm of the service, the horse. The fervid zealots who, like John Bunyan, entered the Parliamentary army, were never in the majority, and needed peculiar training to bring out their remarkable soldierly qualities. The sober, thrifty, religious middle class—which was the backbone of the Parliamentary strength—had no special aptitude for military service. If its members could once be put in the army and kept there a sufficient length of time, their qualities made them excellent soldiers; but, as a whole, they were not men of very adventurous temper, and had had no such training in arms, or in the sports akin to war, as inclined them to rush into the army. On the other hand, the Royalist nobles and squires, and their game-keepers, grooms, and hard-riding kinsmen, with their taste for field-sports, their love of adventure, and their high sense of warlike honor, made splendid material out of which to organize an army, and especially cavalry. In consequence, for the first half of the war the Royalist cavalry was overwhelmingly superior to the Parliamentary cavalry, composed as it was of men bought with the money of the bourgeoisie, who had no particular heart in their work; who were timid horsemen and unskilled swordsmen. The difference in favor of the Royalist horse was as marked as the superiority of the Confederate horse in the American Civil War, under leaders like Stuart, Morgan, and Basil Duke; until time was afforded, in the one case for the growth of Cromwell, in the other for the development of leaders like Sheridan and Wilson.

Cromwell had already shown himself very active. He had seized the magazine of the Castle of Cambridge, and secured the University plate, which was being sent to the King. He had raised volunteers and expended money freely out of his own scanty means. His troop of horse was, from the beginning, utterly different from most of the Parliamentary cavalry; it was composed of his own neighbors, yeomen and small farmers, hard, serious men, whose grim natures were thrilled by the intense earnestness of their leader, and whom he steadily drilled into good horsemanship and swordsmanship. His chaplains always played an important part; one of them, Hugh Peters, was a man of mark, who joined ability to high character.

The King's cavalry was led by Prince Rupert, a dashing swordsman and horseman, a born cavalry leader, who, though only twenty-three, had already learned his trade in the wars of the Continent. Rupert opened the real fighting, scattering a large body of Parliamentary horse in panic rout when he struck them near Powick, on the Severn.

In October the King marched on London, and at Edgehill met the army of Essex. Each side drew up, with the infantry in the centre, the cavalry on the flanks. On the King's side there was much jealousy among the different generals, and some insubordination, but far more activity and eagerness for fight than the Parliamentary troops displayed. The battle was fought on the afternoon of October 23d, and the Parliamentary army was demoralized at the outset by the treacherous desertion of a regiment commanded by a man most inappropriately named Sir Faithful Fortescue. He moved out of the ranks and joined Rupert's horse. Rupert charged with headlong impetuosity, and by his fury and decision so overawed the Parliamentary horse opposed to him that they did not wait the shock, but galloped wildly off, actually dispersing the nearest infantry regiments of their own side. Rupert then showed the characteristic shortcoming which always impaired the effect of his daring prowess. He never could keep his men in hand after they had scattered the foe; he never kept a sufficient reserve with which to meet a counter-stroke. None but a great master of war could withstand his first shock; but after the first shock he was no longer dangerous. At Edgehill his horse followed the routed left wing of the Parliamentarians until they became as completely scattered as their beaten foes. He struck the Parliamentary baggage-train, which was defended by Hampden with a couple of infantry regiments, and his scattered troopers were beaten back when he attempted to take it.

Meanwhile, the Royalist horse of the left wing had fallen with the same headlong fury on the Parliamentary right, but had only struck a small portion of the Parliamentary cavalry. These they drove in rout before them, themselves following in hot pursuit. The result was, that the bulk of the Parliamentary foot, and a portion of the right wing of the Parliamentary horse, including Oliver Cromwell's troop, were left face to face with the Royalist foot, which was inferior in numbers; and falling on it, after a desperate struggle they got the upper hand and forced it back. Rupert at last began to gather his horse together to face the victorious Roundhead foot; and as night fell, the two armies were still fronting each other. The King advanced on London in November, but was unable to force his way into the city, and fell back.

The war had not opened well for the Parliamentary side, and their especial weakness was evidently in cavalry—the arm by which decisive battles in the open field were won. Cromwell, with unerring eye, saw the weakness and started to remedy it. It is about this time that his famous conversation with Hampden took place. Said Cromwell: "Your troops are most of them old decayed serving-men and tapsters, and such kind of fellows; and their troops are gentlemen's sons, younger sons, and persons of quality; do you think that the spirits of such base, mean fellows will ever be able to encounter gentlemen that have honor and courage and resolution in them?... You must get men of a spirit; and take it not ill what I say—I know you will not—of a spirit that is likely to go on as far as gentlemen will go, or else you will be beaten still.... I raised such men as had the fear of God before them, as made some conscience of what they did, and from that day forward they were never beaten."

The famous Presbyterian clergyman, Baxter, who was by no means friendly to Cromwell, described his special care to get religious men into his troop; men of greater intelligence than common soldiers, who enlisted, not for the money, but from an earnest sense of public duty. Naturally, said Baxter, these troopers "having more than ordinary wit and resolution had more than ordinary success."

By another writer of the time, Cromwell's horse are described as "freeholders and freeholders' sons, who upon matter of conscience engaged in this quarrel; and thus being well-armed within by the satisfaction of their own consciences, and without by good iron arms, they would as one man stand firmly and charge desperately." Cromwell at once distinguished himself among his contemporaries, alike by the absolute obedience he rendered to his superiors, and by the incessant, unwearying activity with which he drilled his men in the use of their weapons and horses. He was speedily promoted to a colonelcy. In a news-letter of the time his regiment was described as composed of "brave men; well disciplined. No man swears but he pays his twelvepence; if he be drunk he is set in the stocks or worse; if one calls the other Roundhead, he is cashiered; insomuch that the counties where they come leap for joy of them, and come in and join with them. How happy were it if all the forces were thus disciplined!" Cromwell suppressed all plundering with an iron hand. An eminently practical man, not in the least a theoretical democrat, but imbued with that essence of democracy which prompts a man to recognize his fellows for what they really are, without regard to creed or caste, it speedily became known that under him anyone would have a fair show according to his merits. He realized to the full that the quality of troops was of vastly more consequence than their numbers; that only the best men can be made the best soldiers; and these best men themselves will make but poor soldiers unless they have good training. His troops proved what iron discipline, joined to stern religious enthusiasm, could accomplish; just as later their immense superiority to the forces of the Scotch Covenanters showed that religious and patriotic enthusiasm, by itself, is but a poor substitute for training and discipline. In one of his letters he writes: "I beseech you, be careful what captains of horse you choose; what men be mounted. A few honest men are better than numbers. Some time they must have for exercise. If you choose godly, honest men to be captains of horse, honest men will follow them, and they will be careful to mount such. I had rather have a plain russet-coated captain that knows what he fights for, and loves what he knows, than that which you call a gentleman, and is nothing else. I honor a gentleman that is so indeed.... It may be it provoked some spirit to see such plain men made captains of horse.... Better plain men than none; but best to have men patient of work, faithful and conscientious in employment."

Ordinarily, Cromwell was able to get for his leaders men who were gentlemen in the technical sense of the term, but again and again there forged to the front under him men like Pride, whose natural talents had to supply the place of birth and breeding. He writes again: "My troops increase; I have a lovely company; you would respect them did you know them.... They are honest, sober Christians; they expect to be used as men." Again he writes, when his Presbyterian colleagues were showing a tendency to oppress and drive out of the army men whose religious beliefs did not square with theirs: "Surely, you are not well-advised thus to turn off one so faithful to the cause, and so able to serve you as this man (a certain colonel). Give me leave to tell you I cannot be of your judgment. If a man notorious for wickedness, for oaths, for drinking, hath as great a share in your affection as one who fears an oath, who fears to sin.... Ay, but the man is an 'Anabaptist'! Are you sure of that? Admit he be, shall that render him incapable to serve the public? Sir, the state, in choosing men to serve it, takes no notice of their opinions: if they be willing faithfully to serve it, that satisfies.... Take heed of being sharp or too easily sharpened by others, against those to whom you can object little, but that they square not with you in every opinion concerning matters of religion."

In these sentences lies the justification of genuine democracy, of genuine religious liberty, and toleration by the state of religious differences. They were uttered by a man far in advance of the temper of his age. He was not sufficiently advanced to extend his toleration to Roman Catholics, and even extending it as far as he did he was completely out of touch with the majority of his fellow-countrymen; for the great bulk—both Episcopalians and Presbyterians—were bitterly hostile to the toleration of even inconsiderable differences of doctrine and ritual. The ideal after which Cromwell strove, though lower than that to which we of a more fortunate age have attained, was yet too high to be reached in his day. Nevertheless, it was a good thing to have the standard set up; and once the mark which he had established was reached, it was certain that the spirit of toleration would go much farther. As soon as Baptists and Congregationalists, no less than Episcopalians and Presbyterians, were tolerated by the state for the reasons he gave, it was sure to become impossible to refuse toleration to Catholics and Unitarians.

We must honor Cromwell for his aspirations toward the ideal, but we must acknowledge how far short of reaching it he fell. At this very time he was handling without gloves the Episcopalian clergy. In order to secure the assistance of the Scotch, Parliament had determined to take the Covenant, which made the state religion of England the same form of lofty, but intolerant, Presbyterianism that obtained in Scotland. Under the decision of the Government the ritual of the Church of England was forcibly suppressed, and there was no little harrying of Episcopal clergy and vandal destruction of ancient art symbolism by the Puritan zealots. "Leave off your fooling and come down, sir!" said Cromwell, walking into Ely Cathedral, where the clergyman had persisted in the choir service; and there was no choice but to obey.

In 1643 Cromwell forged to the front as almost the only steadily successful Parliamentary commander. To marvellous energy, fervid zeal, great resourcefulness, fertility of invention, and individual initiative, he added the unerring insight of the born cavalry leader. He soon saw that the true weapon of the cavalryman was the horse; and, discarding the carbines with which his troop had first been armed, he taught them to rely upon the shock of a charging, close-knit mass of men and horses trained to move rapidly as a unit.

He was ceaseless in his efforts to get his men paid, fed, and equipped. Like his great friend, Sir Thomas Fairfax, though he stopped all plundering, he levied heavy fines on the estates of the Royalists, and by these means, and by assessments from the Association, and by voluntary loans and contributions, he was able to keep his men well equipped.

There was no comprehensive strategy in the fighting this year; but the balance of the isolated expeditions undertaken inclined in favor of the King. Cromwell appears clearly, for the first time, as a successful military leader in May, near Grantham. He had under him twelve troops. The Cavaliers much outnumbered him. Nevertheless, when, after some preliminary firing from the dragoons on both sides, Cromwell charged at a round trot, the Cavaliers, instead of meeting the charge, received it and were broken and routed. The fight was of great value as being the first in which the Parliamentary horse beat a superior number of Royalist horse. Cromwell was as yet learning his trade. On this occasion he hesitated a long time about charging, and only charged at all when it became evident that his opponents would not; and he owed his victory to the incompetence of the Royalist commander. It was an invaluable lesson to him.

A great deal of scrambling, confused, and rather pointless warfare followed. Rupert and Hampden encountered each other, and Hampden was defeated and killed. Hampden's great colleague, Pym, died later in the year, just after having brought about the league with Scotland—one of the first-fruits of which was the trial and execution of Laud. Presbyterianism was now dominant, and set itself to enforce everywhere the rigid rule of clerical orthodoxy. Against this the Independents began to raise their voices; but the real force which was to gain them their victory over both Royalist and Presbyterian was as yet hidden. Cromwell's Ironsides—as they were afterward termed when Rupert christened Cromwell himself by that name—the regiments which he raised and drilled after his own manner from the Eastern Association, these represented the real power of the Independents, and these were not yet recognized as the heart and right arm of the army.

Cromwell held Nottingham, where the Royalists attacked him and he beat them off. He took Burleigh House, which was held by a strong Royalist garrison; then, in July, 1643, he advanced to rescue the Parliamentary general, Lord Willoughby, who was besieged at Gainsborough by a division of Newcastle's army. About a mile and a half out of town he met the cavalry of Lord Cavendish, which was drawn up at the top of a hill. To attack him it was necessary to advance up steep slopes, honeycombed by rabbit burrows; but Cromwell's squadrons were already remarkable alike for flexibility and steadiness, and their leader knew both how to prepare his forces and how to take daring advantage of every opportunity that offered. As his leading troops struggled to the top of the hill Cavendish's horsemen advanced, but the Cromwellian troopers, closing up, charged them at once. There was a stiff contest, but as the rest of the Parliamentary troops came to the front, the Royalists were overthrown and driven off in wild rout. Cavendish himself brought up his reserve and routed a portion of the Parliamentary forces; but Cromwell had neither lost his head nor let his force get out of hand. He, too, had a reserve, and with this he charged Cavendish and overthrew him, Cavendish himself being slain.

This feat was succeeded by another quite as notable. After relieving the town and giving Lord Willoughby powder and provisions, Cromwell advanced toward some Royalist soldiers who still remained in view, about a mile distant. To his astonishment, these proved to be the vanguard of Newcastle's whole army, and there was nothing for it but to retreat. Cromwell's troops were tired, and only his excellent generalship and indomitable courage prevented a disastrous rout. Both the Parliamentary horse and foot were at first shaken by the advance of the fresh Royalist soldiery, but Cromwell speedily got them in hand and retired by divisions, making head against the enemy alternately with one body of horse and then with another, while the rest of the troops drew back behind the shield thus afforded them. The alternating squadrons of the rear-guard always made head against the enemy and checked him, but always slipped away before he could charge, and thus the tired army was brought off in safety.

In September Cromwell joined Sir Thomas Fairfax; and in October they met and overthrew a Royalist force at Winceby, the Puritan troopers singing a psalm as they advanced to the combat. The numbers seem to have been about equal, perhaps 3,000 a side. The battle began with a skirmish between the dragoons of the two forces. It was decided by the tremendous charge of Cromwell's steel-clad troopers. The charge was made at the trot, Cromwell leading his men. The Royal dragoons fired upon them as they came on, Cromwell's horse was killed, and a Cavalier knocked him down as he rose, but was himself killed by a Puritan trooper. Cromwell sprang to his feet, flung himself on a fresh horse, and again joined in the fight. His troops were heavy cavalry, cuirassiers, and the opposing Royalists, with only buff coats, were overthrown by the shock of his advance. Fairfax charged in flank, and the rout was complete. The Royalist leaders chronicled with astonishment the fact that the Parliamentary horse showed great superiority—that they were "very good and extraordinarily armed." Apparently the victory was owing to the excellent drilling of Cromwell's troops, which enabled them to charge knee to knee; and when thus charging, the weight of the horses and of the ironclad men made them irresistible.

In 1644 the war at first dragged on as a series of isolated expeditions and fights in which neither side was able to score any decided advantage. Rupert performed two or three brilliant feats; the Scotch crossed the border to aid the Parliamentarians; and Charles tried to come to some understanding with the Irish, by which they would, if possible, furnish him troops, and if not, would at least free the English troops in Ireland. Some of the latter he did bring over. After one or two successes a body of them were captured and many subscribed to the Covenant. The most noted man who thus changed sides was the after-time General, George Monk.

Cromwell was looming up steadily; not only for the discipline of his men, but for the vigilant way in which he kept touch with the enemy and gained information about them, making the best possible use of pickets, outposts, and scouting parties; all, by the way, being, as was usual in those times, under the headship of an officer known as the Scout-master—a far better term than the cumbrous modern "Chief of the Bureau of Intelligence." Of course Cromwell's growing military reputation added greatly to his weight in Parliament, of which, like most of the leading generals, he was still a member. His first feat during this year showed how little the duties of the soldier and the statesman were as yet differentiated.

Early in January he appeared in the House of Commons, charged Lord Willoughby with misconduct, and brought about his removal and the naming of Manchester to the sole command in the seven associated counties. Manchester was little more than a figure-head. He made Cromwell his lieutenant-general and yielded in all things to him, until he was alienated by falling under the control of the Scotch Covenanters, who already hated Cromwell as a representative of the "sectaries" whom they persecuted. The House of Commons appointed a Committee of Both Kingdoms to assume the supreme executive authority for the conduct of the war. Cromwell was made a member of this Committee, and was also the ruling member of the Committee of the Eastern Association, which furnished the zealously Puritan force that was already the mainspring of the Parliamentary army.

In June the Scotch, under the Earl of Leven, and the English, under Lord Fairfax and Lord Manchester, were besieging York, which was defended by Lord Newcastle. Toward the very last of the month Rupert marched rapidly to its relief. The three Parliamentary generals fell back instead of falling on him as he advanced. Newcastle wished to leave them alone, but Rupert insisted upon following and attacking the Parliamentary armies. He and Newcastle had about 20,000 men. The Parliamentarians probably numbered some 25,000; but throughout this war it is impossible to give either the numbers or the losses with accuracy.

On July 2d Rupert overtook the end of the Parliamentary column, which was saved from disaster only by the fortunate fact that the horse of Cromwell and Sir Thomas Fairfax formed the rear-guard. The two latter sent on word of Rupert's advance, warning the Parliamentary generals that they could not now avoid a fight; and promptly the Scotch and English troops were turned to face their Royalist foes on Marston Moor.

A ditch stretched across the moor, and the armies drew up with this extending for most of its length between them. Each side was marshalled in the usual order—infantry in the centre, cavalry on the flanks. The horse of the Parliamentary right wing was commanded by Sir Thomas Fairfax, who had under him his own English cavalry and three Scottish regiments. The right wing of the foot was commanded by Lord Fairfax, and consisted of the Yorkshire troops and two brigades of Scots. The centre, with its reserve, consisted of Scotch troops; the left, of the infantry of the Eastern Association. Leven was with the infantry of the centre; Manchester on his left. The horse of the left wing were under Cromwell, his Ironsides occupying the front line with three Scotch regiments in reserve.

In the Royalist army the horse on the left wing were under Goring; the infantry in the centre were under Newcastle, and Rupert himself led the horse of the right wing. At last the two great cavalry leaders of the war—Rupert and Cromwell—were to meet face to face. The war had lasted nearly two years. The best troops, under the best leaders, had reached very nearly their limit of perfectibility; they were veterans, soldiers in every sense.

Hour after hour passed while the armies stood motionless, the leaders on either side anxiously scanning the enemy, seeking to find a weak point at which to strike. Evening drew on and no move was made. The Royalist leaders made up their mind that the battle would not be fought that day. Suddenly, at seven o'clock, the whole Parliamentary army moved forward, the Puritan troopers chanting a psalm, according to their wont.

On the right, Fairfax's troopers, as they advanced, were thrown into disorder. Goring charged them furiously, drove them back on the reserve of Scotch cavalry, and overthrew them all. The rout was hopeless, and the flying horsemen carried away the Yorkshire foot with them. Sir Thomas kept the ground, with a few of his troopers and a large number of Lord Balgony's Scotch Lancers and the Earl of Eglinton's Scotch Cuirassiers. The fugitives were followed in hot pursuit by Goring, but part of his horse were kept in hand by their commander, Sir Charles Lucas, who, wheeling to the right, charged the flank of the Scotch foot, who had formed the Parliamentary centre, and who had now crossed the ditch and were attacking the Royalists in front. The Scotch fought with stubborn valor, repulsing Lucas again and again, but suffering so heavily themselves that it became evident that they could not long stand the combined front and flank attack.

While disaster had thus overtaken the Parliamentary right, on the left Cromwell had completely the upper hand. His steel-clad troopers crashed into Rupert's horsemen at full speed. The fight was equal for some time, neither stubborn Roundhead nor gallant Cavalier being able to wrest the mastery from the other. But Rupert, who always depended upon one smashing blow, and put his main force into his front line, did not, like Cromwell, understand how best to use a reserve. Cromwell's reserve—the Scotch cavalry—came up and charged home, and the Royalist horse were overthrown with the shock. "God made them as stubble to our swords," said Cromwell.

Sending his leading troops in pursuit, to prevent the enemy from rallying, Cromwell instantly gathered the bulk of his horse and fell on the right wing of the Royalist foot—already hard pressed by the foot of the Eastern Association. The King's men fought with dogged courage, most conspicuous among them being Newcastle's own Northumbrian Regiment, the famous Whitecoats, who literally died as they stood in the ranks.

Sweeping down the line the Ironsides smashed one regiment

after another, until, in the fading summer evening, Cromwell had almost circled the Royalist army, and came to their left wing, where he saw the Royalist horse charging the right flank of the Scots and harrying the routed Yorkshire foot. Immediately he reformed his thoroughly trained squadrons almost on the same ground where Goring's horse stood at the beginning of the battle, and fronting the same way. The foot of the Association formed beside them, and just before nightfall the Puritan cavalry and infantry made their final charge. Goring's troopers were returning from their pursuit; Lucas's men were recoiling from their last charge, in which Lucas himself had been captured. They were scattered like chaff by the shock of the steel-clad Cromwellian troopers, riding boot to boot; and the remaining Royalist foot shared the same fate. The battle was over just as night fell, stopping all pursuit. But there was little need of pursuit. As at Waterloo, the very obstinacy with which the fight had been waged made the overthrow all the more complete when at last it came. Night went down on a scene of wild confusion, with thousands of fugitives from both armies streaming off the field through the darkness; for the disaster to the right wing of the Parliamentary army had resulted not only in the rout of all the Yorkshire men and half of the Scotch, but also in the three Parliamentary commanding generals, Leven, Manchester, and Lord Fairfax, being swept off in the mass of fugitives. The fight had been won by Cromwell, not only by the valor, coolness, keen insight, and power of control over his men, which he had showed in the battle itself, but by the two years of careful preparation and drill which had tempered the splendid weapons he used so well.

This was the first great victory of the war; but it produced no decisive effect; for there was no one general to take advantage of it. York fell; but little else resulted from the triumph. Fairfax, Manchester, and Leven all separated to pursue various unimportant objects. They left Rupert time to recruit his shattered forces. They did not march south to help Essex, who was opposed to the King in person. Essex blundered badly, and when he marched into Cornwall was out-manœuvred and surrounded, and finally had to surrender all his infantry. Before this the King had already beaten the Parliamentary general, Waller, at Copredy Bridge, the defeat of the Parliamentarians being turned into disaster by the conduct of the London trained-bands, who, after two years of battle, were still mere militia, insubordinate and prone to desert. It was not with such stuff that victory over the Royalists could be obtained. Mere militia who will not submit to rigid discipline cannot be made the equals of regulars by no matter how many years of desultory fighting. In the War of the American Revolution it was the Continentals—the regulars of Washington, Wayne, and Greene—who finally won the victory, while even to the very end of the struggle the ordinary militia proved utterly unable to face the red-coats. So in the English Civil War, it was the carefully drilled and trained horse and foot of the Eastern Association, and not the disorderly London trained-bands, who overthrew the King's men. Cromwell had developed his troops just as Grant and Lee, Sherman and Johnston long afterward developed theirs. It is only under exceptional conditions, and with wholly exceptional populations, that it is possible to forego such careful drilling and training.

One great reason for the failures of the Parliamentary forces was that their leading generals no longer greatly cared for success. They were Presbyterians, who believed in the Parliament, but who also believed in the throne. They hated the Independents quite as much as they hated the Episcopalians, and felt a growing distrust of Cromwell, who in religious matters was the leader of the Independents, and who had announced that if he met the King in battle he would kill him as quickly as he would kill anyone else. Essex was no more capable of putting a finish to the war than McClellan was capable of overthrowing the Confederacy. The one, like the other, had to make room for sterner and more resolute men.

The Committee of both Kingdoms struggled in vain to get their generals to accomplish something. At Newbury—where one indecisive battle had already been fought—they got together an army nearly double the strength of the King's: with no result save that another indecisive battle was fought, on October 29,

1644. It was evident that there had to be a complete change in the management of the war if a victory was to be achieved. Accordingly Cromwell once more turned from the field to the House of Commons.

In November he rose in Parliament and denounced Manchester as utterly inefficient; and then turned his onslaught from an attack on one man into a general move against all the hitherto leaders of the army. On December 9th he addressed the House in one of his characteristic speeches, rugged in form, but instinct with the man's eager, strong personality, fiery earnestness and hard common-sense. He pointed out, not all the truth—for that was not politic—but the evident truth that it was not wise to have leaders who both served in Parliament and also commanded in the army. The result was the passage of the Self-denying Ordinance, by which all members of either of the Houses were required to resign their commands; so that, at a stroke, the Presbyterian and Parliamentary leaders were removed from their control of the forces. Two months afterward it was decreed that the forces of the Commonwealth should be reorganized on the "New Model." For the short-time service and militia levy system there was substituted the New Model; that is, the plan under which in the Eastern Association the Ironsides had been raised to such a pitch of efficiency was extended to include the whole army. Sir Thomas Fairfax was put in command, but so evident was it to everyone that Cromwell was the real master-mind of the Parliamentary armies that the Self-denying Ordinance was not enforced as far as he was concerned, and he was retained, nominally as second, but in reality as chief, in command. This was not only a victory for the radical military party, but a victory for the Independents over the Presbyterians. The Independent strength was in the army, and they now had their own leaders.

During the period of reorganization of the army the war lagged along in its usual fashion, with Rupert as much to the fore as ever; and to the Royalists it merely seemed that their adversaries had gotten at odds, and that the great noblemen, the experienced leaders, had been driven from their leadership. Their hopes were high, especially as in Scotland affairs had taken a sudden and most unexpected turn in their favor. Immediately after Marston Moor Montrose had begun his wonderful year of crowded life. Recognizing the extraordinary military qualities of the Celtic clansmen of the Highlands, he had stirred them to revolt, and had proved himself a master of war by a succession of startling victories which finally put almost all Scotland at his feet. One would have to examine the campaigns of Forrest to find any parallel for what he did. Because of his feats he has been compared to Cromwell, but his fights were on so much smaller a scale that the comparison is no more possible than it would be possible to compare Forrest with Grant or Lee.

It is a noteworthy fact that the two soldier types which emerged from the English Civil War as victorious over all others were the Cromwellian Ironside and the Scotch Highlander. The intense religious and patriotic fervor and hard common-sense of the one was in the other supplanted by a mere wild love of fighting for fighting's sake. It may be questioned which was most formidable in battle, but in a campaign there was no comparison whatsoever between them; and once his other foes were vanquished, the Cromwellian soldier had not the slightest difficulty in holding down the Highlander.

The victories of Montrose, the feats of Rupert, and the failures of the Parliamentarians since Marston Moor gave Charles every feeling of confidence, when, on June 14, 1645, he led his army against the New Model at Naseby. As usual in these battles, it is not possible to state the exact numbers, but it would appear that, as at Marston Moor, the Royalists troops were outnumbered, being about 10,000 as against 14,000 in the Parliamentary army. Fairfax commanded for the Parliament, and the King was present in person. As usual, the infantry on each side was in the centre. On the right wing of the Parliamentarians Cromwell led his horse, while Ireton had the horse of the left. Rupert commanded the cavalry on the right wing of the Royalists, and Sir Marmaduke Langdale that of the left. Thus Rupert was not, as at Marston Moor, pitted against Cromwell; and anyone except Cromwell he could beat. Ireton was a stout soldier, but he and his cavalry were completely overthrown; then, according to their usual custom, Rupert's Cavaliers followed the headlong flight of their opponents in an equally headlong pursuit. Meanwhile, in the centre, the foot crashed together and fought with savage obstinacy on equal terms. As at Marston Moor, the fight was decided solely by Cromwell. He overthrew the Royalist horse as he always overthrew them, and he kept his men in hand as he always kept them. Leaving a sufficient force to watch the broken hostile squadrons, he wheeled the remainder and fell on the Royalist infantry in flank and rear. For a moment, King Charles, stirred by a noble impulse, led forward his horse guards to do or die; but the Earl of Carnworth seized his bridle and stopped him, saying: "Will you go upon your death?" Had the King been indeed a king, as ready to stake his own life for his kingdom as he was to stake the lives of others, it would have gone hard with the man who sought to halt him, for in such a case no man is stopped by another unless he himself is more than willing; but Charles faltered, the moment passed, and his army was overthrown in wild ruin. Rupert came back and reformed his men, but when Cromwell charged home with horse and foot the Royalist troopers never waited the onslaught. There was plenty of light for pursuit now, and Cromwell showed yet another trait of the great commanders by the unsparing energy with which he followed his foe to complete the wreck. For twelve miles the Parliamentary horse kept touch with the flying foe. The King's army was hopelessly shattered; from half to two-thirds of their number were slain or captured. The Parliamentary losses were also heavy; a thousand of their men were killed or wounded. Ireton had been wounded, and Skippon, the Parliamentary major-general of foot. Fairfax, who had behaved with his usual gallantry, had had his helmet knocked off in the hand-to-hand fighting. The victory was Cromwell's.

So decisive was the overthrow that it practically ended the war. For a moment the King had hopes of what Montrose would do; but when Montrose came out of the Highlands he found that the clansmen would not march beside him for a long campaign; at

Philiphaugh he was overwhelmed by numbers, and the Royalist party in Scotland disappeared with his overthrow. Fairfax whipped Goring and captured Bristol. Cromwell took Winchester, where he dealt severely with certain of his troopers who had been plundering. He then stormed Basing House, an immense fortified pile, the property of the Catholic Marquis of Winchester. Again and again the Parliamentary generals had attempted to take the place, but had always been beaten. Cromwell would not be denied; after three days' battering with his guns, and an evening spent in prayer and in reading the 115th Psalm, he stormed it with a rush, and the splendid castle, its rooms and galleries filled with all the treasures of art, was left a blackened and blood-stained ruin. After this it was in vain that the Royalist troops strove to make head against their foes. If they stood in the open they were beaten; castle after castle, and fortified manor-house after manor-house, were battered down or stormed by Cromwell and his comrades; and in the spring of 1646 the King surrendered himself to the Scotch army.

III. THE SECOND CIVIL WAR AND THE DEATH OF THE KING

When the stout old Royalist, Sir Jacob Astley, was overcome and surrendered, he exclaimed, as he gave up his sword: "Now you have done your work and may go play, unless you fall out among yourselves!" It very soon became evident that the victors would fall out among themselves. Any revolutionary movement must be carried through by parties whose aims are so different, or whose feelings and interests are so divergent, that there is great difficulty in the victors coming to a working agreement to conserve the fruits of their victory. Not only the leaders, but more especially their followers—that is, the mass of the people—must possess great moderation and good sense for this to be possible. Otherwise, after much warfare of factions, some strong man, a Cromwell or a Napoleon, is forced or forces himself to the front and saves the factions from destroying one another by laying his iron hand on all.

In the middle of the seventeenth century the English people, accustomed for many generations to look to the monarch as their real ruler, began to tumble into chaos when they wrenched themselves free from the ingrained hereditary habit which had made loyalty to the King and orderly government convertible terms. They were not yet fit to govern themselves unaided; such fitness is not a God-given, natural right, but comes to a race only through the slow growth of centuries, and then only to those races which possess an immense reserve fund of strength, common-sense, and morality. The English of the middle of the seventeenth century were very much farther advanced along the road than were the French at the end of the eighteenth. They had no such dreadful wrongs to avenge as had the French people, and they indulged in no such bloodthirsty antics among themselves. But they had by no means attained to that power of compromise which they showed forty years later in the Revolution of 1688, or which was displayed by their blood-kin and political heirs, the American victors in the struggles of 1776 and 1861. In the English Revolution that placed William on the throne, in the American Revolution, and in the American Civil War, the victors passed through periods of great danger when it seemed possible that the fruits of their victory might be thrown away. They did not suffer the fate of the victors of 1648, chiefly because of the growth of the spirit of tolerance, of the capacity for compromise, which enabled them in part to ignore their own differences, and in part to abide by a peaceful settlement of them.

In England, by 1688, the Cromwellian movement had itself educated even those who most sincerely believed that they abhorred it; and there was a far less servile spirit toward James II. than toward Charles I. There was less fanatical intolerance of one another among the elements that had combined to put William on the throne; and William, otherwise by no means as great a man as Cromwell, was yet far more willing to accept working compromises, and more content to let Parliament go its own way, even when that way was not the wisest. After the American Revolution Washington's greatness of character, sound common-sense, and entirely disinterested patriotism, made him a bulwark both against anarchy and against despotism coming in the name of a safeguard against anarchy; and the people were fit for self-government, adding to their fierce jealousy of tyranny a reluctant and by no means whole-hearted, but genuine, admission that it could be averted only by coming to an agreement among themselves. Washington would not let his officers try to make him Dictator, nor allow the Continental Army to march against the weak Congress which distrusted it, was ungrateful to it, and refused to provide for it. Unlike Cromwell, he saw that the safety of the people lay in working out their own salvation, even though they showed much wrong-headedness and blindness, not merely to morality, but to their own interests; and, in the long run, the people justified this trust.

But Cromwell never wanted the people to decide for themselves, unless they decided in the way that he thought right; and, on the other hand, the difficulty with the people was even greater; for they had neither the desire for freedom, the moderation in using freedom, nor the toleration of differences of opinion, which the American colonists had developed by the end of the following century. At the close of, and after, the American Civil War the differences of opinion and belief among the victors were such as would inevitably have produced further fighting in Cromwell's time. The Northern Democrats were anxious to combine politically with the defeated Southerners, and to reinstate, as nearly as might be, the old ante-bellum conditions—that is, to prepare for another Civil War. The Republican Party itself showed signs of a deep division between the Extremists and Moderates, while there were all sorts of violent little factions, just as there were Anabaptists and Fifth Monarchy men in Cromwell's time. The Garrison or disunion Abolitionists, for instance, had formed just such a faction, and had seen their cause triumph, not through, but in spite of, their own efforts. If the Abolitionists of the Wendell Phillips type, instead of seeking to compass Lincoln's defeat for the Presidency in 1864 by peaceful means, had threatened armed agitation; if, instead of trying to elect McClellan or Seymour at the polls, the Northern Democrats had taken the field with the former at their head; if the Republicans had first crushed them by force of arms, and then had fought among themselves until the extreme radical element got the upper hand, installed Grant as perpetual President and dissolved Congress when it became evident that the Democrats and moderate Republicans combined would outnumber the radicals—we should have had a very fair analogy to what happened in the Cromwellian era.

In such a case, moreover, be it remembered that the fault would have lain less with the perpetual President than with the people whose defects called him into being. Cromwell did not stand on the lofty plane of Washington; but, morally, he was infinitely and beyond all comparison above the class of utterly selfish and unscrupulous usurpers, of whom Napoleon is the greatest representative. At the close of the first Civil War there is no reason to suppose that he had any ambition inconsistent with the highest good of his country, or any thought of making himself paramount. To all outward seeming, his efforts were conscientiously directed to securing the fruits of the victory for liberty, while at the same time securing stability in the government. Unfortunately, in coming to an agreement among men, no moderation or wisdom on the part of any one man will suffice. Something of these qualities must be possessed by all parties to the agreement. The incurable treachery of King Charles rendered it hopeless to work with him; and the utter inability of Episcopalians, Presbyterians, Roman Catholics, and indeed of all parties and all creeds to act on the live-and-let-live principle, rendered a really free government almost unworkable at the moment. How little Cromwell yet thought of striving for a kingly position is shown by his conduct in his social relations, notably by the marriages of his children, who at this time sought their mates in families of his own rank. The only one of these marriages with which we need concern ourselves is that of his daughter, Bridget, to Ireton, a good soldier and able politician, who was devoted to Cromwell, and was on very close and intimate terms with him.

The religious element entered into everything Cromwell did, mixing curiously with his hard common-sense and practical appreciation of worldly benefits. It appears in all his letters and speeches. Such a letter as he wrote to the Speaker of the House after the storming of Bristol, is in thought and manner more akin to the writings of some old Hebrew prophet than to those of any conqueror before or after Cromwell's time. It is saturated, not merely with biblical phraseology, but with biblical feeling, all the glory being ascribed to God, and the army claiming as their sole honor that God had vouchsafed to use them in his service, and that by faith and prayer they had obtained the favor of the Most High. It is impossible for a fair-minded and earnest man to read Cromwell's letters and reports after action, and the prayers he made and the psalms he chose to read and to give out before action, and to doubt the intensity of the man's religious fervor. In our day such utterances would be hypocritical. Almost the only modern generals in whom they would have been the sincere expression of inward belief were Stonewall Jackson and Gordon; and the times had changed so utterly that even they could not possibly give utterance to them as Cromwell did. But in Cromwell's time the most earnest Puritans thought as he did, and expressed their thoughts as he did. That such expression should lend itself very readily to hypocrisy was inevitable; indeed, it was perhaps inevitable that the habitual use of such expression should breed somewhat of hypocrisy in almost any user. The incessant employment by Cromwell and his comrades of the word "saints," to distinguish themselves and those who thought like them, is particularly objectionable in its offensive self-consciousness.

In this letter about the taking of Bristol Cromwell touches upon the religious differences which were the great causes of division among the victors. He writes:

"Presbyterians, Independents, all have here the same spirit of faith and prayer; the same presence and answer; they agree here; have no names of difference; pity it is it should be otherwise anywhere.... And for brethren in things of the mind we look for no compulsion but that of light and reason."

Cromwell strove earnestly to bring about harmony between the Independents of the New Model army and the Presbyterians, who were dominant in Parliament. Even in that day there were in private life men of high character and great intellect who believed in true religious liberty, men who stood far ahead of Cromwell; but Cromwell was equally far ahead of all the men who then had any real control in public life; so far ahead, indeed, that he could not get any considerable body of public opinion abreast of him.

The Ironsides, the cavalry of Cromwell, stood as the extreme representatives of the spirit which actuated the army. The great bulk of them were men of intense political and religious convictions. However, many even of the cavalry, and a large majority of the rank and file of the infantry, were of the ordinary military type, men of no particular convictions, a considerable number, indeed, having been enlisted from among the captured armies and garrisons of the King himself. Under the ties of discipline and comradeship, such men were sure to follow with entire fidelity the masterful spirits among the officers and in their own ranks; and all these masterful spirits were devoted to Cromwell as the great leader who had given them victory. They were even more devoted to their conceptions of religious and political liberty, and were resolutely bent on striking down the King who embodied, in their minds, the principles of religious and political oppression. These men had broken entirely with the past, and were no longer overawed by the name of hereditary power. "What," they asked, "were the Lords of England but William the Conqueror's Colonels, or the Barons but his Majors, or the Knights but his Captains?"

They believed they were indeed the Lord's chosen people, and that upon them, as conquerors, there devolved the duty of safeguarding the interests of religion and of the Commonwealth. They wished to strike down the Bishops as well as the King; and though most of them were Congregationalists or Baptists, they had already begun to develop plenty of men whose Christianity was of the most heterodox form, or who boldly announced that they had a right to profess any creed, Christian or otherwise, if they so desired. Together with their iron discipline as an army went wide liberty of thought and discussion on all outside matters—religious and political alike—when they were not in the ranks. There were preachers who served with sombre fidelity as privates, but who were fanatical inciters of Republican enthusiasm in every leisure hour, haranguing and exhorting their fellow-soldiers about every political or religious wrong.

Trouble was brewing between this army and Parliament. The Episcopalians—the Royalists—had left Parliament when the war broke out. The Presbyterians were in complete command. London, which held the purse-strings of the Parliamentary cause, was strongly Presbyterian. Now, the Presbyterians, as the war went on, had grown more and more afraid of their allies, and, indeed, of too decisive a victory over the King. They were just as much bent upon an intolerant uniformity in Church matters as was Laud, though they wished to substitute a different form of Church government, which should rest upon a broader and more popular basis. They wished to make Parliament supreme, but they had no idea of dispensing with the King, and they were exceedingly distrustful of a popular movement which would extend liberty beyond and beneath the classes from which they drew their strength. On the contrary, the army, which represented the Independent movement, was strongly democratic in its tendencies, and was filled with sullen wrath against the King.

Cromwell himself was no theorist; in fact, he was altogether too little of one. He wished to do away with concrete acts of oppression and injustice; he sought to make life easier for any who suffered tangible wrong. Though earnestly bent upon doing justice as he saw it, and desirous to secure the essentials of liberty for the people as a whole, he failed to see that questions of form—that is, of law—in securing liberty might be themselves essential instead of, as they seemed to him, non-essential. He was reluctant to enter into general schemes of betterment, especially if they seemed in any way visionary. But when his feelings were greatly roused over specific cases of wrong-doing or oppression, he sometimes became so wrought up as to advocate reform in language so sweeping that he seemed to commit himself, not only to absolute religious toleration, but to complete political equality. Thus when he broke with Lord Manchester he told him that he hoped "to live to see never a nobleman in England." In open Parliament he denounced "monarchical government." He advocated entire religious freedom. In dealing with the army he declared his readiness to maintain the doctrine that "the foundation and the supremacy is in the people—radically in them—and to be set down by them in their representations"—that is, by their representatives in Parliament.

Of course, to make his conduct square with these various utterances, Cromwell would have had to strive for precisely such a government as Washington was able to inaugurate a century and a half later; a government in which there should be complete religious toleration, in which all differences of rank and title should be abolished, and in which the basis of representation in Parliament would have to approach more or less closely to manhood suffrage. Doubtless, there were times when Cromwell ardently wished for such a Government; but it was wholly out of the question to realize it in the middle of the seventeenth century, even in England. Generations had to pass before men could grasp the true principles of religious toleration and political equality in all their bearings; and, like every other man who actually works out great reforms, who actually does signal service in the world, Cromwell had to face facts as they were, and not as bodies of extremists—no matter how good—thought they ought to be.

The best and most high-minded of the Puritan party were now growing to fear lest the Presbyterians should try to perpetuate the old religious oppression under a new name. Milton—with but one exception the greatest poet of the English tongue, a man whose political and social ideas were at least two centuries in advance of his time, but who had the good sense to accept, no matter with what heart-burning, the best possible when he could not get the best—Milton expressed the convictions of his whole party when he said that if "Presbyter was but Priest writ large" the people were no better off than before.

The army began to show openly its spirit of fierce unrest. A very considerable portion avowed extreme republican theories. The Levellers, as they were called, were looked upon in that day, even by advocates of freedom like Cromwell, with great distrust, although the principles they advocated—such as manhood suffrage—are now the commonplaces of American politics. Of course, then they were not commonplaces; they were revolutionary ideas, for the reception of which the mind of the English people was not ready, and therefore it was the duty of men who sought practical reform to refuse to put these schemes into operation.

There were much more extreme and dangerous groups than the mere Republicans; groups of men in whom the desire for religious, political, and moral reform had overstepped the broad, but not always clearly marked, border line which divides sane and healthy fervor from fanaticism. In such troublous times small sects and parties of extremists swarm. Already the foundations were laid for the Fifth Monarchy men, the men who believed that the times were ripe for the installation of the last great world monarchy, the monarchy of which the Saviour himself was to be Ruler; the men who shouted for King Jesus, and were ferociously opposed to everybody who would not advocate the immediate introduction into all mundane affairs of Heaven's law, as the Fifth Monarchy men chose to interpret it. Of course, men of this type are always to be found in every free government, and aside from their peculiar notions, they may have excellent traits. In peaceful times and places like the United States at the present day, they merely join little extreme parties, and run small, separate tickets on election-day, thereby giving aid, comfort, and amusement to the totally unregenerate. In times of great political convulsion, when the appeal to arms has been made, these harmless bodies may draft into their ranks—as the Fifth Monarchy men did—fierce and dangerous spirits, ever ready to smite down with any weapons the possible good, because it is not the impossible best. When this occurs they need to be narrowly watched.

There are many good people who find it difficult to keep in mind the obvious fact that, while extremists are sometimes men who are in advance of their age, more often they are men who are not in advance at all, but simply to one side or the other of a great movement, or even lagging behind it, or trying to pilot it in the wrong direction.

The seething unrest of the army found expression in the creation of a regular political organization to oppose the organized Parliament. The officers formed a Council, and the rank and file chose delegates, two for each company or troop, known as "agitators." In short, the army became an organized political body whose scarcely acknowledged function was to control or supersede the Parliament; just as, prior to the outbreak of the American Revolution, Committees of Correspondence were formed, in the various colonies, out of which there sprang the Continental Congress, which superseded the loyalist colonial legislatures.

Cromwell, like every other great leader who rises in a period of storm and convulsion, could partly direct the forces around him, and in part had to be directed by them. He did not sympathize with the extreme position of the army about the King—the "man of blood," as the Puritan zealots called him, whose life they already demanded; nor yet with their radical political aspirations. But it was the army alone through which he could act, which gave him his strength; and in return he was the one man who could in any way check or control it, for its loyalty to, and admiration of, the great leader at whose hands it had drained the cup of victory, were the only emotions strong enough to offset its fierce zeal for its own theories of Church and State.

Cromwell was most earnestly desirous of getting a working compromise between the King, the Presbyterian Parliament, and the Independent army; a compromise which would allow the King to reign, exercising such executive powers as the Parliament felt he should possess, and which should leave the supreme control to Parliament, but with sufficient guarantees for political and religious freedom to insure justice to the Independents and the soldiers. He strove so hard to accomplish his purpose as to excite angry mutterings against himself among his own followers in the army; and the first steps of the impending revolution were seemingly taken by him only because he was irresistibly pushed onward by the army itself. When, however, he had once made up his mind that there was no other path possible, he trod it as a leader, with all his wonted firmness and decision.

The effort for reconciliation was hopeless, chiefly because the King was an utterly impossible person with whom to deal. He had many bitter foes; but they could not prevail against him until he convinced some of his would-be friends that he was absolutely and utterly untrustworthy. He never for a moment entertained the idea of accepting his defeat, of abandoning the effort to rule as a despot, and of acting with good faith toward the people. His purpose was to play off the Presbyterians, together with the Scotch, against the Independents; as he wrote to a friend, he hoped to get either the one party or the other "to side with me for extirpating one another, and I shall be really King again."

Meanwhile, the Presbyterian Parliament was determined not

to tolerate the "sectaries" of the Congregationalist and Baptist Churches, and was drawing closer and closer to the Scotch Covenanters, who were even more intolerant; and finally it grew ready to accept the King himself on almost any terms, if it could overcome the army.

But the army could not be overcome. It had perfected its political organization, and had begun to work through Ireton—Cromwell's other self. The army was genuinely reluctant to break with the Parliament, for, after all, it was deeply permeated with the English respect for law and order; and in the elections to fill the vacancies in the House, very many Independents—men like Ireton, Fairfax, and Blake, the after-time admiral—had been returned, so that there was in the Parliament a party which strongly sympathized with the army.

The majority in Parliament, however, remained steadfast in its own views, and by its refusal to give the soldiers their arrears of pay it added a very tangible, material grievance to those of an ethical character. In January, 1647, the Scottish army delivered King Charles to the agents of the Parliament, and quitted England, having received part of the sum of money due them.

The most complicated and devious negotiations followed between the King, the Parliament, and the army. Cromwell tried to get the army in touch with the Parliament, but found the Parliament hopelessly obstinate. He tried to get it in touch with the King, but found the King hopelessly false. Yet, neither could the King and Parliament come together. Then the army threatened mutiny, whereupon the Parliament began to negotiate for bringing back the Scottish force to overawe the New Model, and attempted the disbandment of the latter. The army struck back with great decision and sent Cornet Joyce to seize the person of the King and take him away from the Presbyterians. Parliament attempted to proceed with the disbandment of the army, but was forced to abandon the effort when it became evident that to pursue it meant war. No one knew quite what the outcome would be, or, indeed, what his own course would be.

Cromwell, like the rest, was drifting; he seriously thought of leaving England and going to Germany to fight for the Protestant cause, as the Thirty Years' War had not yet come quite to an end. To the French ambassador, who sounded him on the object of his ambition, he answered: "No one rises so high as he who knows not whither he is going." He was certainly at this time making the most honest efforts to come to an agreement, either with the King, or the Parliament, or with both, provided only liberty of conscience should be granted, the power of Parliament guaranteed against the despotism of the King, and the rights of the people guaranteed as against the despotism of Parliament. But, when Parliament began to negotiate with the Scots on its account, and Charles secretly sought to enter into a separate agreement with the Scots on his account, to bring about an invasion of England, while the city mob, which was rabidly Presbyterian, forced the hand of the House of Commons and compelled its members to defy the army, it became evident that Oliver had to choose his course. Reluctantly he was pushed along the road of military revolution. The speaker and the Independent members of Parliament, in fear of the London mob, took refuge with the army, whither Cromwell himself had already gone. On June 10th the army issued a manifesto, demanding a settlement of the difficulties upon terms which it approved. Early in August it marched in formidable and orderly parade through the city, overawing resistance by its mere appearance, and Parliament submitted. This was the real beginning of the military interference which terminated in the military dictatorship of one man. If Cromwell is to be blamed for what he did to the Long Parliament, this is the step for which he is to be blamed most; yet it was a step approved by Milton, Fairfax, Ireton, and the great majority of the best and most high-minded believers in English liberty who were then alive. The conduct of the King and the Parliament had been such that it is difficult to see how any other course was possible.

Cromwell did his best to stop the Revolution at the point it had now reached. For months he endeavored to make terms with the King on the conditions outlined above; and he not only put a stop to the extreme democratic agitation of the Levellers and refused to further the plan for a republican commonwealth, but, with prompt severity, repressed a mutiny that broke out under the cry of "England's Freedom and Soldiers' Rights." He disregarded the grumbling of the army until he became convinced that Charles was incurably false, incurably treacherous and untrustworthy, and was fomenting a counter-revolution. Then Cromwell turned from him with loathing, and made up his mind to trust to the sword, and to strike down anyone, even the King himself, if the need warranted it.

It was high time for action. In Ireland the Royalists, the Catholics, and even the Presbyterians, were uniting against the Parliament. The Scotch, under the lead of Hamilton and the Presbyterian Royalists, declared for the King; the English Presbyterians were for him to the extent that they were against the army; and throughout England the Cavaliers were arming for an uprising. Dark indeed seemed the peril. It had taken four years for the English Presbyterians, the Scotch, and the New Model, the army of the Independents, to conquer the Royalists, and now the New Model was pitted single-handed against the Scotch and the Royalists, while the Presbyterians were at best lukewarm. Nevertheless, exactly as in the French Revolution, the victory lay with the Mountain when it was brought face to face not only with hostile parties in France but with the rest of armed Europe, so now the fierce energy of the New Model, with the greatest of Englishmen at its head, was destined to prove too much for its foes. The grim Ironsides rallied to their cause with the devotion of fanatics, and the well-ordered discipline of splendid soldiers. With fierce exhortations and sermons, with internal searchings of spirit, with outpourings of prayer, they made ready for battle, and in each dark Puritan heart welled the determination not only to put down armed resistance, but to take the last great vengeance upon the King, the cause of the blood-guiltiness.

In April, 1648, the Second Civil War broke out. The gentry of Wales were a unit for the King, and the commonalty followed them. The Cavaliers rose in force in the North, and the Scotch prepared to send a formidable army across the border to their aid; and there were Royalist outbreaks everywhere, even in the southern and eastern counties. Berwick, Carlyle, Chester, Pembroke, Colchester, were seized and held for the King. The Presbyterians of London were in commotion; the Presbyterians in Parliament itself were half-hearted and divided; but the Independents and the army had no doubts. Fairfax marched into Kent and Essex, and, after some hard fighting, trampled under foot the insurrection. One Parliamentary Colonel whipped the Welsh at St. Fagan's; another crushed out a Royalist rising in Lancashire; General Lambert was sent to the North, where Sir Marmaduke Langdale—Oliver's old foe at Naseby—had raised Yorkshire for the King. Oliver himself marched to the siege of Pembroke, which, owing to lack of cannon, he could not take until July 11th. This ended the Welsh War. The risings in the south and centre had been thoroughly stamped out; the fleet, which had partially revolted, was for the most part brought back to loyalty; and there remained only to deal with the Northern Royalists and the Scotch army under the Duke of Hamilton, which had by this time crossed the border.

The composition of Hamilton's army and the history of events in both Scotland and Ireland at this moment, are alike sufficient to show the tangle in which politics then were—the kaleidoscopic changes in the relations of factions and parties, and the seeming minuteness of the points of difference over which these same parties waged ferocious and resolute war. Hamilton's cavalry was commanded by Munro, who had come over from Ulster to take part in the invasion of England. Munro and the Scotch Presbyterians of Ulster had, during the years immediately succeeding the great Irish uprising, been the formidable and merciless opponents of the Irish of the North. But when the English Civil War was fairly on, the English Royalists in Ireland—Episcopalians and Catholics alike—gradually lost their animosity toward their Irish foes, in their greater animosity toward the Puritans, and finally the Presbyterians followed suit. This resulted in the release of Munro and a large part of the Presbyterian force in Ulster, who went to the aid of Hamilton. Hamilton's own government was Presbyterian and ostentatiously devoted to the Covenant. It is very difficult for a modern observer to see any essential point of difference, either in their attitude toward the Covenant, toward the King, or toward England; between the party that at the moment controlled Scotland, and the party which was soon to drive it out of power. Yet the bitterness between them was intense. The bulk of the Presbyterian ministers, and the fiercest and most intense Presbyterian zealots, hated Hamilton and his fellows with mortal hatred, and were only waiting their chance to rise against them.

Cromwell advanced to the encounter with entire confidence, and sternly anxious to get at his foes. He was a thorough Englishman at a time when, to the thorough Englishman, the Scotch were classed with other aliens. Bitterly though he hated the Royalists, he yet acknowledged them as fellow-countrymen; but he made no such acknowledgment in the case of the Scots. He explained that he preferred the Cavalier interest to the Scottish interest, just as he preferred the Scottish to the Irish; and he now moved against enemies whom he regarded not merely as enemies to his cause, but as enemies to his country.

There seemed every reason for the Scots to be confident. Even with their help the Parliamentarians had been able to put down the Royalists only at the cost of four years of hard fighting; and now the Scotch and the Royalists were to act together. They were to be pitted against Cromwell, the best Parliamentary commander, to be sure; but the Scotch had done at least as well as the average of the allies at the victory of Marston Moor, and still had in mind the memory of their easy successes against their English foes in the two Bishops' Wars.

The great victories of the Parliamentary army had hitherto been won when the odds in numbers were in their favor; now, they were about to fight with the odds over two to one against them. Hamilton's army was about 21,000 strong, including 3,000 Yorkshire Royalists under Langdale. Cromwell had only some 9,000 men; but the great bulk of them were veterans, who under his leadership had become the finest soldiers of the age.

Hamilton moved slowly south toward Preston, his army scattered in a long line, Langdale at the head, and Munro bringing up the rear. Cromwell abandoned his heavy baggage-train that it might not encumber his movements; Lambert joined him, and he marched with fiery speed to strike his foes. The Scotch, confident in their numbers, and ignorant of the movements of their speedy antagonist, advanced in loose order. On August 17th Cromwell struck their army; by which time Hamilton's straggling march had resulted in Langdale's taking position to cover its left flank. The Scotch were partially aware of their danger and were uneasily trying to concentrate. Langdale was left to bear the shock of the first attack single-handed. Cromwell appreciated, as well as any commander that ever lived, the vital element of time; the need for taking full advantage of what the moment brought forth. His headlong march had resulted in some of his soldiers lagging behind the others, but he had gained what he wanted; he had surprised his foes when they were unprepared to use their superiority of force, and he dashed at them as soon as his foremost men came up, determined to destroy them in detail. Langdale made a stiff fight, and owing to the character of the country—the fields were small, and the fences strong and high—the cavalry was not able to do much, so that the decisive fighting was done by the infantry, which was not usually the case in these wars. The struggle took place about four miles from Preston, near which town, but south of the river Ribble, the bulk of the Scotch foot were gathered.

For four hours Langdale's men clung to their hedges and buildings, regiment after regiment of the Cromwellians fighting to dislodge them. Says Cromwell: "Our men fought with incredible valor and resolution ... often coming to push of Pike, and to close Fire, and always making the Enemy to recoil ... the Enemy making, though he was still worsted, very stiff and sturdy resistance. Colonel Dean's and Colonel Pride's, outwinging the enemy, could not come to so much share of the Action ... the Enemy shogging down toward the Bridge, and keeping almost all in reserve that so he might bring fresh commands often to fight."

The Scotch sent some men and ammunition to Langdale, but made no serious effort to help him, and continued their march. At last he was overpowered and driven into the town. As soon as his men were dislodged from the hedges and enclosures, the

Cromwellian horse fell furiously upon them, utterly routing and scattering them; at the same time, the Cromwellian foot, pushing forward, drove back the Scotch foot, which had been posted near the bridge to secure a passage for Langdale across the Ribble, and cut off the fugitives from the rest of the army.

The Ironsides thundered into the streets of Preston at the heels of Langdale and the flying remnants of his forces. Hamilton led one or two charges, and for a moment checked the pursuit, but it was now too late to retrieve matters, and soon afterward the whole of his army was again in panic rout. The beaten cavalry fled north, goaded by the Cromwellian sword, until they reached the rear guard under Munro. Most of the Yorkshire and Scotch infantry north of the Ribble were killed, captured, or scattered; a few only escaped to the Scotch army south of the Ribble by swimming across it.

The day thus ended with the defeat of part of the Scotch forces, who lost in killed or captured, 5,000 men, besides those who were dispersed. Moreover, the Scotch army was cut in two; Munro being to the north, separated from all the rest, who, under Hamilton, were completely cut off from their base in Scotland. Sending a few troops to harry the flying horsemen, Cromwell turned to deal with the Scotch main army, which was even yet more numerous than his own. But the Scotch were cowed by the success of Cromwell's utterly unexpected attack. The soldiers had lost confidence in their leaders, and they were cut off from their own country, and, therefore, from all hope of supplies. A council of war was held that night, and the retreat was continued. The fagged-out Cromwellians followed and harassed them. The horse, under Colonel Thornhaugh, rode into their rear ranks and bothered and detained them, though at cost of the life of the Colonel, who was shot in one of the fierce struggles. Again and again the Scotch stood, but each time to be beaten; the last stand being made at Winwick church, under a "little spark in a blue bonnet" who himself was slain. Here they lined the hedges with musketeers, and filled the lane with their pikemen, and hours went by before the Puritans, under Pride, finally pushed their charge home, and gained possession of the place which had been held so stubbornly. Both sides were utterly worn out, and it was impossible to urge the pursuit as rapidly and strongly as Cromwell hoped. Finally, leaving Lambert to deal with the shattered fragments of Hamilton's command, Cromwell turned north and followed Munro.

The victory was overwhelming. Two thousand Scotch and Royalists had been slain, and 10,000 were captured; more than Cromwell's whole force. Almost all the generals were taken; Hamilton was afterward beheaded. The fate of the captured rank and file was hard. Throughout the First Civil War, the common soldiers, when taken, had either been exchanged or released, or often enough had enlisted on the side of the victors; but the Puritan generals and those behind them were in no mood to take a merciful view of men whom they regarded as wanton offenders, whether they were Scotchmen or Englishmen. The captives of Preston battle were sold into slavery; some being sent to the Virginia planters, and others to the Venetian Government, for galley slaves. When the Puritans could act thus toward their fellow-Englishmen, and toward the Scotch Presbyterians who were so nearly of their own creed, there is small cause for wonder in the treatment afterward accorded the Irish. It was a merciless age, the age of Tilly and Wallenstein, and we cannot judge its great men by the canons of to-day.

This was the first time that Cromwell had actually been in supreme command in a great victory, and too much praise cannot be accorded him for his hardihood, energy, and skill. The speed of his motions and his prompt decision had rendered it possible for him to strike home at his adversary in the flank, and to eat him up piecemeal. During three days of incessant marching and fighting he halted only to do battle or to take the rest absolutely needed; and at the end of that time the enemy's foot had been killed, captured, or dispersed to the last man, and his horse was a beaten rabble, flying toward the border.

The battle of Preston put an end to the Second Civil War. Colchester capitulated to Fairfax immediately afterward. The part of the fleet that had revolted had come back under Prince Charles and Rupert, to coöperate with the risen Royalists, but could do nothing; most of the ships in time returned to their allegiance to the Parliament. The indomitable Rupert, with seven ships, kept the sea and made a long cruise, which finally degenerated into mere buccaneering. Blake, whom the Parliament made Admiral, pursued him, captured most of his ships, and finally forced him to take refuge in France. In Scotland, Argyle and the Presbyterian ministers—the Kirk party—on the news of Hamilton's overthrow, promptly rose in the so-called Whigamore raid. Munro fell back, plundering right and left until he crossed the border.

Cromwell's exertions had been so severe that he could not follow the flying Royalists with his usual rapidity. The army had been long without pay; they had not a penny with which to get their horses shod, and so many horses had been slain and were lamed or done out that a large number of the troopers were on foot, and the others could hardly spur their jaded mounts into a trot. Munro was not only a ruthless plunderer, but a hard fighter, and on his arrival in Scotland Argyle felt doubtful as to his capacity to cope with him, and sent to Cromwell for assistance. Cromwell promptly invaded Scotland, being careful to pose as the ally of Argyle and the Kirk, and therefore the true friend of the Scottish nation. According to his custom, he rigorously suppressed plundering. All resistance withered away before him. He was received at Edinburgh as a powerful and honored ally, and before he recrossed the border the Scotch were again avowed supporters, for the time being at least, of the Parliament.

The enemy in arms had been defeated. It remained to deal with the Parliament and the Presbyterian party. Some had been active for the King; most had been lukewarm; the victory had been a victory for the army, and therefore for the Independents. Neither Cromwell nor the army was of a temper to refrain from finishing matters. Before the struggle was decided Cromwell had written Fairfax: "I pray God teach this nation and those that are over us ... what the mind of God may be in all this, and what our duty is. Surely it is not that the poor, godly people of this Kingdom should still be made the object of wrath and anger, nor that our God would have our necks under a yoke of bondage. For these things that have lately come to pass have been the wonderful works of God, breaking the rod of the oppressor."

He was not in the least a doctrinaire Republican or Parliamentarian; he believed as little in the divine right of majorities as in the divine right of kings. Neither would he have admitted such a right as existing in an army, or, as yet, in himself. But it was impossible to stand still. He had to act with some party, though with none was he in entire accord; for one was hostile, another hopelessly undecided, the third prone to extreme measures and representing only a minority in the nation. He could only act with the last, and yet this meant an overturn of the recognized governmental authorities. Whether he would or not, he had to proceed along the path of revolution.

The Presbyterians—the men who controlled Parliament—were halting between two burdens. They would not push far enough against the King to make the Revolution a success, or to put a permanent end to despotism; and they would not eat their past words and deeds by turning wholly to his support. The King himself was obstinately bent on keeping the supreme power in his hands and setting the people under his feet, whatever he might promise; and this was the attitude of the large Royalist and Episcopalian party, which had showed, in supporting him, either that it cared little for liberty and eagerly championed a servility which it misnamed loyalty, or else that it feared disorder more than tyranny.

On the other hand, the determined foes of Absolutism, the armed Independents, were even more cut off from the bulk of the nation by their good qualities than by their shortcomings. Their advocacy of toleration for every creed, their desire for legal reform, and their strong democratic tendencies, all put them so far in advance of the rest of the nation as to be completely out of touch with it; and they offended it even more than their harshness and narrowness, and the behavior of the bands of fantastic enthusiasts in their ranks. Moreover, the sincerity of their convictions, at a time when the practical application of belief in the rule of the majority was entirely new and strange, drove them to rely on their strong right arms, instead of upon the votes of a people which was mainly hostile or apathetic. When Cromwell acted with them, heedless of what the majority might think, he was making ready for a time when he might choose in turn to disregard the majority within their own ranks.

Though neither Cromwell nor the Independents believed in the abstract in employing the army as an instrument of government, they were face to face with a condition of affairs in which, partly because of their own shortcomings, but very much more because of the shortcomings of their antagonists, they were driven to adopt this as the only possible course. Doubtless Cromwell was still acting as he sincerely believed the interests of the nation demanded. In the complex tissue of motives which go to determine a man's deeds it is rarely possible to say that there is not some, and mayhap even a strong, element of self-interest and of desire for personal aggrandizement; yet Cromwell's conduct toward the King goes to show that he would gladly have saved him had not the behavior of this typical Stuart been such as to render it impossible for an upright and far-seeing friend of English liberty longer to remain his ally.

Parliament had no sooner been relieved by the action of the army from all danger from the King's adherents, than in September it proceeded to open negotiations with the King. These negotiations in effect aimed at the destruction of the army by uniting Parliament and King against it; among other things, they expressly excluded any toleration for the sects which made up the strength of the army. It would have been inexcusable folly for the men who had won the victory to submit to such action. The army, headed by Ireton, demanded a purge of the House which would rid it of the members so treacherous to the interests of the nation. Ireton and his followers then laid before Fairfax a remonstrance, which included a demand that the King should be brought to justice for the "treason," "blood," and "mischief" of which he had been guilty. Fairfax opposed this and carried the army with him in favor of a substitute which merely requested the King to assent to a constitutional plan which would have limited his powers precisely as those of Queen Victoria are now limited, and would have made the Constitution of England what it now is. A more moderate proposal was never made by victorious revolutionists, and it shows conclusively that the fault was not with Cromwell and his followers when they were forced to overturn the King and the Parliament. But Charles promptly rejected the proposals and thereby signed his own death-warrant. He had just sought, in Cromwell's words, "to vassalize us to a foreign nation," and now, after having twice plunged England into Civil War, and shown himself eager to submit her to the power of the alien, he obstinately refused a plan which would not merely have left him unpunished, but would have given him all the power of a constitutional monarch; a power greater than that which the House of Orange at that time enjoyed in Holland.

The House of Commons stood firm in its position, and against the position of the army, which thereupon marched into London; and on December 6th, Colonel Pride carried through the famous "Pride's Purge." He stood with a military guard at the door of the House, and turned back or arrested the members who had voted for a continuation of the negotiations with the the King. This was, of course, a purely revolutionary measure, with no warrant, save as Ireton and Harrison—the Republican generals—had said, "the height of necessity to save the Kingdom from a new War." It was but the second step; the all-important one had been taken long before, when the army first marched into London to see that the Parliament did its liking.

Cromwell still strove to save the King's life. Through the exertions of Ireton a small majority of the army council resolved for mercy, and made a last effort to conclude a treaty with the King; but the King would not listen to them, and he thus put it out of their power any longer to delay his fate. On January 1, 1649, the House of Commons resolved to try him for treason to the kingdom. The Lords refused to pass the ordinance, whereupon the House of Commons decided to disregard them and to act on its own authority. On January 6th it erected a High Court of Justice for the trial of the King, on the ground that he had wickedly endeavored to subvert the people's rights, had levied war against them, and when he had been spared had again raised new commotions in order to enslave and destroy the nation. Cromwell had finally thrown his doubts to the winds, and he supported the resolution with all his vigor. When the legality of the action was questioned, he retorted: "I tell you we will cut off his head with the crown upon it!" The grim Puritan leaders were at last to have their will on "the man of blood." On the 27th, sentence of death was passed upon the King, and on January 30, 1649, he was beheaded on the scaffold in front of Whitehall, meeting his death with firm dignity.

Justice was certainly done, and until the death-penalty is abolished for all malefactors, we need waste scant sympathy on the man who so hated the upholders of freedom that his vengeance against Eliot could be satisfied only with Eliot's death; who so utterly lacked loyalty that he signed the death-warrant of Strafford when Strafford had merely done his bidding; who had made the blood of Englishmen flow like water, to establish his right to rule as he saw best over their lives and property; and who, with incurable duplicity, incurable double-dealing, had sought to turn the generosity of his victorious foes to their own hurt.

Any man who has ever had anything to do with the infliction of the death-penalty, or indeed with any form of punishment, knows that there are sentimental beings so constituted that their sympathies are always most keenly aroused on behalf of the offender who pays the penalty for a deed of peculiar atrocity. The explanation probably is that the more conspicuous the crime, the more their attention is arrested, and the more acute their manifestations of sympathy become. At the time when the great bulk even of civilized mankind believed in the right of a king, not merely to rule, but to oppress, the action of the Puritans struck horror throughout Europe. Even Republican Holland was stirred to condemnation, and as the King was the symbol of the State, and as custom dies hard, generations passed during which the great majority of good and loyal, but not particularly far-sighted or deep-thinking men, spoke with intense sympathy of Charles, and with the most sincere horror of the regicides, especially Cromwell. This feeling was most natural then. It may be admitted to be natural in certain Englishmen, even at the present day. But what shall we say of Americans who now take the same view; who erect stained-glass windows in a Philadelphia church to the memory of the "Royal Martyr," or in New York or Boston hold absurd festivals in his praise?

The best men in England approved the execution of the King, not only as a work of necessity, but as right on moral grounds. Two weeks after the execution, Milton—perhaps the loftiest soul in the whole Puritan party, full though it was of lofty souls—wrote his pamphlet justifying the right of the nation to depose, or, if need be, execute, tyrants and wicked kings. His arguments never have been, and never can be, successfully controverted on grounds of justice and morality. There is room for greater question on the ground of expediency. Some of the ablest historians and politicians have argued that the execution was a mistake, as making the King a martyr, and as transferring to his son, Charles II., all the loyalty that had been his, while the hatred and distrust could not be transferred. Yet, it certainly seems that even on the score of expediency, Cromwell and the regicides were right and that the event justified their judgment. While Charles was alive there could have been no peace in any event; and during Cromwell's lifetime Charles II. could gain no foothold in England—for there was never a member of the House of Stuart that could stand in battle or in council before the stern Lord of the English Commonwealth. If in later years great Oliver could only have managed to agree with the bulk of liberty-loving Englishmen on some system of government by law, it is not probable that the memory of the King's death would have prevented the perpetuation of such a government.

Carlyle's mind is often warped; his vision often dim; but there are times when he speaks like an inspired seer, and never more so than when dealing with the execution of the Stuart King: "This action of the English Regicides did in effect strike a damp like death through the heart of Flunkyism universally in this world. Whereof Flunkyism, Cant, Cloth-Worship, or whatever ugly name it have, has gone about incurably sick ever since; and is now at length, in these generations, very rapidly dying. The like of which action will not be needed for a thousand years again.... Thus ends the Second Civil War. In Regicide; in a Commonwealth, and Keepers of the Liberties of England. In punishment of delinquents; in abolition of Cobwebs—if it be possible in a Government of Heroism and Veracity; at lowest of Anti-Flunkyism, Anti-Cant, and the endeavor after Heroism and Veracity."

IV. THE IRISH AND SCOTCH WARS

The successful Revolutionary party now enacted that the people of England and of all the dominions and territories thereunto belonging were constituted and established as a Commonwealth, or Free State, to be governed by the representatives of the people in Parliament and by whomsoever the Parliament should appoint as officers and ministers; the King and the House of Lords being both abolished. No provision was at first made by which any man should lawfully be recognized as chief in the new Commonwealth; but, as a matter of fact, there was one man, and one man only, who had to be acknowledged, however unwillingly, as master and leader. There were many upright and able civil servants; many high-minded and fervent reformers; many grim and good captains: but waist-high above them all rose the mighty and strenuous figure of Oliver Cromwell. It may well be that, hitherto, personal ambition had played an entirely subordinate part in all his actions. Now, in the turmoil of the Revolution, in the whirlpool of currents which none but the strongest man could breast, he became ever more and more conscious of his own great powers—powers which he knew were shared by no other man. With the sense of power came the overmastering desire to seize and wield it.

The first thing he had to do was to stop the Revolution where it was. In every such Revolution some of the original adherents of the movement drop off at each stage, feeling that it has gone too far; and at every halt the extremists insist on further progress. As stage succeeds stage, these extremists become a constantly diminishing body, and the irritation and alarm of the growing remainder increase. If the movement is not checked at the right moment by the good sense and moderation of the people themselves, or if some master-spirit does not appear, the extremists carry it ever farther forward until it provokes the most violent reaction; and when the master-spirit does stop it, he has to guard against both the men who think it has gone too far, and the men who think it has not gone far enough.

The extreme Levellers, the extreme Republicans, and, above all, the fierce and moody fanatics who sought after an impossible, and for the matter of that a highly undesirable, realization of their ideal of God's kingdom on this earth—all these, together with the mere men of unsettled minds and the believers in what we now call communism, socialism, and nihilism, were darkly threatening the new government.

Men arose who called themselves prophets of new social and religious dispensations; and every wild theory found its fanatic advocates, ready at any moment to turn from advocacy to action. In the name of political and social liberty, some demanded that all men should be made free and equal by abolishing money and houses, living in tents, and dividing all food and clothing alike. In the name of religious reform others took to riding naked in the market-place, "for a sign"; to shouting for the advent of King Jesus; or to breaking up church services by noisy controversies with the preachers. The extreme Anabaptist and Quaker agitators were overshadowed by fantastic figures whose followers hailed them as incarnations of the Most High.

Black trouble gloomed without. The Commonwealth had not a friend in Europe. In the British Isles Scotland declared for Charles II. as the King, not only of Scotland, but of Great Britain. In Ireland but a couple of towns were held for the Parliament.

It was to the reconquest of Ireland that the Commonwealth first addressed itself, and naturally Cromwell was chosen for the work. He was given the rank of Lieutenant-General; but before he started he had to deal with dangerous mutinies and uprisings in the army. The religious sectaries and political levellers, who had given to the army the fiery zeal that made it irresistible by Parliament or King, English Royalists or Scotch Covenanter, had also been infected with a spirit peculiarly liable to catch flame from such agitations as were going on roundabout. Here and there, in regiment after regiment, were sudden upliftings of the banner of revolt in the name of every kind of human freedom, and often of some fierce religious doctrine quite incompatible with human freedom. Cromwell acted with his usual terrible energy, scattered the mutineers, shot the ringleaders, and reduced army and kingdom alike to obedience and order. Then he made ready for the invasion of Ireland.

The predominant motives for the various mutinies in the army, offer sufficient proof of its utter unlikeness to any other army. At the outset of the civil wars the Ironsides were simply volunteers of the very highest type; not wholly unlike, at least in moral qualities, some of those belated Cromwellians—the Boers of to-day. They did not take up soldiering as a profession, but primarily to achieve certain definite moral objects. Of course, as the force gradually grew into a permanent body, it changed in some respects; but the old spirit remained strong. The soldiers became in a sense regulars; but they bore no resemblance to regulars of the ordinary type—to regulars such as served under Turenne or Marlborough, Frederick the Great or Wellington. If in Grant's army a very large number of the men, including almost all the forceful, natural leaders, had been of the stamp of Ossawatomie Brown, we should have had an army much like Cromwell's. Such an army might usually be a power for good and sometimes a power for evil; but under all circumstances, when controlled by a master hand, it was certain to show itself one of the most formidable weapons ever forged in the workshop of human passion and purpose.

Matters in Ireland were in a perfect welter of confusion. Eight years had elapsed since the original rising of the native Irish. A murderous and butcherly warfare had been carried on throughout these years, but not along the lines of original division. On the contrary, when Cromwell landed, there had been a complete shifting of the parties to the contest, every faction having in turn fought every other faction, and, more extraordinary still, having at some time or other joined its religious foes in attacking a rival faction of its own creed. The original rising was in Ulster, and was aimed at the English and Scotch settlers who had been planted under James in the lands from which the Irish had been evicted.

These "plantations" under James, not to speak of the scourge of Wentworth under Charles, were on a par with the whole conduct of the English toward Ireland for generations, and gave as ample a justification for the uprising as in the Netherlands the Spaniards had given the Dutch. From the stand-point of the Irish, the war was simply the most righteous of wars—for hearthstone, for Church, and for country.

This first uprising was one of Celtic Catholics. In the Pale and elsewhere, here and there throughout Ireland, were large numbers of Old-English Catholics; these, unlike the Celts, did not wish separation from England, but did wish complete religious liberty for themselves, and, if possible, Catholic supremacy. The Episcopalian and Royalist English throughout Ireland, under the lead of the Earl of Ormond, favored the King. The Puritan oligarchy of Dublin favored the Parliament, and were in touch with the Scotch Presbyterians of Ulster. The rising began to spread from Ulster southward. The Catholics of the Pale were at first loyal to the King, but the Protestant leaders, in striking back at the insurgents, harried friend and foe alike, until the Pale joined with Ulster. After this, all Ireland revolted. Only a few fortified and garrisoned towns were held for the English.

Violent alterations of policy and of fortune followed. Under the lead of the Roman Catholic clergy the revolt was consolidated. Unswerving loyalty to the King was proclaimed, war was denounced against the Puritans, and the re-establishment of Roman Catholicism as the State religion of Ireland was demanded. On the Puritan side the lords justices in Dublin nominally acknowledged the King's authority, but really stood for the Parliament and hampered Ormond, who, while a stanch Protestant, was an ardent Royalist. Ormond gained one or two victories over the insurgents in spite of the way in which the lords justices interfered with him. Charles created him marquis, and he took command of the English interest, drove out the lords justices, and concluded a truce for one year with the Catholic party, in September, 1643. They gave Charles a free contribution of £30,000, and sent over some Irish troops to aid Montrose and the other Royalist leaders in Scotland, besides setting Ormond free to transfer part of his forces to the King in England. But Munro and the Ulster Scotch refused to recognize the armistice, took the Covenant, and declared against the King; while, in the south, certain Protestant sea-coast towns, under the lead of Lord Inchiquin, followed suit and acknowledged the Parliament. Months of tortuous negotiations followed, King Charles showing the same readiness in promise, and utter indifference in performance, while dealing with the Irish as while dealing with the English. The treachery of the King was made manifest by the discovery of his secret treaty with the Irish, when Sligo was captured.

Meanwhile, the Papal nuncio, an Italian, had arrived, and exhorted the Irish to refuse any peace with the King except on the basis of the complete reinstatement of the Catholic Church. He roused what would now be called the ultramontanes against the moderate Catholic party which was acting with Ormond. Their wrangles caused a fatal delay, for by the time the moderates triumphed the King had been made a prisoner. Their treaty of peace with the King was not signed till September, 1645, and it amounted to nothing, for the adherents of the Parliament rejected it on the one side, and the extreme Catholic party, the utterly intolerant and fanatical Catholics, under the nuncio, refused to be bound by it on the other. In the north the Irish were led by Owen O'Neil, a member of the great Ulster house of that name, and under him they had beaten Munro and the Scotch. He now hurried to the support of the nuncio. The moderate Catholic leaders and Ormond fled to Dublin at his approach, and he was joined, after some hesitation, by Preston, the leader of the Irish forces in the south. In 1647, Ormond, at his wits' end, handed over Dublin to the agents of the Parliament, and joined the Royalist refugees in France.

This for a moment eliminated the Royalists, and left the party of the nuncio, the party of the bigots and intolerant extremists, supreme among the Irish. But when Jones, the Puritan leader, marched out of Dublin and defeated Preston, while in the south Lord Inchiquin won some butchering victories, the party of the moderates again raised its head. Then there was a new and bewildering turn of the kaleidoscope. Inchiquin suddenly became offended with the Parliament, made overtures to Preston, and then to Ormond. A coalition was formed between the Royalist Protestants in Munster and the moderate Catholics. The nuncio threatened the moderates with excommunication and interdict, and fled to O'Neil's camp. Preston and Inchiquin joined forces and marched against O'Neil, so that civil war broke out among the insurgents themselves.

Colonel Jones, the victor over Preston, felt doubtful of his own troops, who included a number of Royalists, and, extraordinary to relate, he actually made terms with the nuncio and O'Neil as against the Protestant Royalists and moderate Catholics—the Ultramontanes so hating the moderate Catholics that they preferred to come to terms with the Puritans. Ormond now came over from France to head the moderates, the party of the Royalist Catholics and Protestants. Peace was declared between Ormond and the Supreme Council of Dublin in the King's name.

But hardly had peace been declared when news arrived of the King's execution. Ormond proclaimed Charles II., at Cork; most of the Irish outside of Ulster united under him, and Munro and the Scotch Presbyterians joined him. The nuncio fled the country in despair. The rupture between the Presbyterians and Independents was complete, and the Scotch became the open enemies of the English. They began the siege of Derry, which Coote held for the Parliament. At the same time they confronted O'Neil and the Ulster Irish, who were acting in alliance with Monk, who held Dundalk for the Parliament by order of Colonel Jones. Inchiquin captured Drogheda for the Confederates. Monk's garrison mutinied, and he had to surrender Dundalk. Ormond began the siege of Dublin, but was routed by Jones, one of the sturdiest of the many sturdy Puritan fighters. Meanwhile, the Puritan Parliament had disavowed the alliance with O'Neil and the Ulster Irish, and the latter were thus forced into the arms of Ormond, who found himself at the head of all the Irish and English Catholics, of the Scotch Presbyterians in Ulster, and of the Royalist Protestants elsewhere in Ireland. It was at this time that Cromwell landed.

The exact condition of affairs in Ireland should be carefully borne in mind, because it is often alleged, in excuse of Cromwell's merciless massacres, that he was acting with the same justification that the English had when they put down the Indian Mutiny with righteous and proper severity. Without a doubt, Cromwell and most Englishmen felt this way; and in the case of the average Englishman, who could not be expected to understand the faction-fighting, the feeling was justifiable. But it was Cromwell's business to know what the parties had been doing. As a matter of fact, the wrong of the original Ulster massacre, which itself avenged prior wrongs by the invaders, had been overlaid by countless other massacres committed by English and Irish alike, during the intervening years; and the very men against whom this original wrong had been committed were now fighting side by side with the wrong-doers, against Cromwell and the Puritans. Moreover, for some time the Parliamentarians had been in close alliance with these same wrong-doers against the moderate Irish, who were not implicated in the massacres in question, and against the Royalist Protestants, some of whom had suffered from the massacres and others of whom had helped avenge them. The troops against whom Cromwell was to fight were in part Protestant and English, these being mixed in with the Catholics and Irish; and at the moment the chief Royalist leaders in Ireland included quite as many English, Scotch, and Irish Protestants, as they did Irish Catholics.

Cromwell recked but little of nice distinctions between the different stripes of Royalists and Catholics when, in August, 1649, he landed in Dublin, the only place in Ireland, save Derry, which still held out for the Parliament. He brought with him the pick of his troops and soon had at Dublin some 10,000 foot and 5,000 horse. They were excellently disciplined; they included the Ironsides, the veterans of the New Model—grim Puritans for the most part, inflamed with the most bitter hatred against Catholics, Irish, and Royalists. They had been welded into one formidable mass by Cromwell's rigid discipline, and yet were all aflame with religious and political enthusiasm. There could not be gathered in all Ireland an army capable of meeting in the open field that iron soldiery, under such a leader as Cromwell; and this the Irish chiefs well knew.

Cromwell, therefore, had to deal with a numerous and individually brave but badly disciplined enemy, formidable in guerilla warfare, because theirs was a wild country of mountain and bog, and resolute in defence of their walled towns, but not otherwise to be feared by such troops as the Ironsides. His first care was to put an end to the plundering and licentiousness which had hitherto marked the English no less than the Irish armies. He completely stopped outrages upon the peasantry and non-combatants generally, besides protecting all who lived quietly in their homes.

In September he marched against Drogheda, into which Ormond had thrown 3,000 picked men, largely English, under Sir Arthur Aston. Cromwell had with him some 8,000 men when he sat down to attack it. He brought up a siege-train, beating back the sallies of the garrison with ease, and meanwhile maintaining his strict discipline, and putting down pillage by the summary process of hanging the plunderers.

When his batteries were ready he summoned the Governor to surrender, but the summons was refused. For two days the guns kept up their fire, and then in the afternoon the assault was delivered. The defenders met the stormers in the breaches; the fight was hot and stiff; the English were once repulsed, but came forward again and carried the breach only to be once more driven out by a fierce rally.

When Cromwell saw his men driven down the breach, he placed himself at the head of the reserve, and in person led it with the rallied men of the broken regiments, back to the breach. This time the stormers would not be denied. They carried the breach, the church—which was strongly held by the Irish—and finally the palisaded intrenchments of Mill Mount, in which Sir Arthur Aston had taken refuge. The horse followed close behind the foot, and speedily cleared the streets of the hostile cavalry and infantry. The victorious Puritans pressed on and a terrible slaughter followed. Cromwell forbade them to spare any that were in arms in the town, and they put to the sword over 2,000 men. Nearly 1,000 were killed in the great Church of St. Peter's. "All the priests found," says Cromwell, "were knocked on the head promiscuously but two, both of whom were killed next day." Sir Arthur Aston, Verney, the son of the King's standard-bearer at Edgehill, and all the officers were put to the sword. Two towers held out until next day, when they submitted; their officers were "knocked on the head," says Cromwell. One tower fought hard; there every tenth man of the soldiers was killed; the rest, and all the soldiers in the other tower, were shipped to the white slavery of the Barbadoes. Of the assailants, about a hundred were slain and several hundred wounded.

Said Cromwell: "We put to the sword the whole number of the defendants.... This hath been a marvellous great mercy. I wish that all honest hearts may give glory of this to God alone, to whom indeed the praise of this mercy belongs.... I am persuaded that this is a righteous judgment of God upon these barbarous wretches who have imbrued their hands in so much innocent blood, and that it will tend to prevent the effusion of blood for the future, which are the satisfactory grounds to such actions, which otherwise cannot but work remorse and regret. The officers and soldiers of this garrison were the flower of their army."

Cromwell's defenders say simply that he acted from a fervent belief in the righteousness of what he was doing, and, further, that the terrible vengeance he took here and at Wexford upon all who withstood him in arms cowed the Irish and prevented further resistance. Neither defence is tenable. If on the ground of their sincerity the deeds of Cromwell and his soldiers at Drogheda and Wexford can be defended, then we cannot refuse the same defence to Philip and Alva and their soldiers in the Netherlands. Of course, we must always remember that under Cromwell there was no burning at the stake, no dreadful torture in cold blood; and, therefore, at his worst, he rises in degree above Philip and Alva. But in kind, his deeds in Ireland were the same as theirs in the Netherlands; and though the Puritan soldiers were guiltless of the hideous licentiousness shown by the Spaniards, or by the armies of Tilly and Wallenstein, yet the merciless butchery of the entire garrisons and of all the priests—accompanied by the slaughter of other non-combatants, in at least some cases—leave Drogheda and Wexford as black and terrible stains on Cromwell's character. Nor is there any justification for them on the ground that they put a stop to resistance. The war lingered on for two or three years in spite of them; and in any event the outcome was inevitable. It does not seem to have been hastened in any way by this display of savagery. There had been many such butcheries during the war, before Cromwell came to Ireland, without in any way hastening the end. Cromwell and his lieutenants put down the insurrection and established order because they gained such sweeping victories, not because Cromwell made merciless use of his first victories. It was the fighting of the Puritan troops in the battle itself which won, and not their ferocity after the battle; and it was Cromwell who not merely gave free rein to this ferocity, but inspired it. Seemingly quarter would have been freely given had it not been for his commands. Neither in morals nor in policy were these slaughters justifiable. Moreover, it must be remembered that the men slaughtered were entirely guiltless of the original massacres in Ulster.

Immediately after Drogheda, Cromwell sent forces to Dundalk, which was held by the Irish, and to Trim, which was held by the Scotch; but the garrisons deserted both places at the approach of the Cromwellians. In October, Cromwell himself advanced on Wexford and stormed the town. Very little resistance was made, but some 2,000 of the defenders were put to the sword. This time the soldiers needed no order with reference to refusing quarter; they acted of their own accord, and many of the townspeople suffered with the garrison. Practically, the town was depopulated, not one in twenty of the inhabitants being left.

Then Cromwell moved to Ross. In spite of the slaughter which he made in the towns he stormed, he exercised such strict discipline over his army in the field, and paid with such rigid punctuality for all supplies which the country people brought in, that they flocked to him as they feared to do to their own armies, and in consequence his troops were better fed and able to march more rapidly than was the case with the Irish. He soon took Ross, allowing the garrison to march out with the honors of war, and gave protection to the inhabitants. When asked to guarantee freedom of religion he responded: "For that which you mention concerning liberty of conscience, I meddle not with any man's conscience. But, if by liberty of conscience, you mean liberty to exercise the mass, I judge it best to use plain dealing, and to let you know, where the Parliament of England have power, that will not be allowed of."

Three months after he landed, Cromwell had possession of almost all the eastern coast. One of the remarkable features of his campaign had been the way in which he had used the army and the fleet in combination. He used his admirals just as he had used his generals and colonels, and they played a very important part in the operations against Wexford and Ross, and in securing the surrender of both. When he moved away from the coast his task was very difficult; there were no roads, the country had been harried into a wilderness, and was studded with castles and fortified towns, every one held by an Irish garrison. Ormond and O'Neil were in the field with a more numerous force than his; and though they dared not fight a pitched battle, they threatened his detachments. The service was very wearing, and in December Cromwell went into winter quarters, the weather being bad, and his men decimated by fever. The triumphs won by his terrible soldiership rendered the conquest of the whole island only a question of time.

Having now a little leisure, Cromwell published, for the benefit of the Irish, a "Declaration," as an answer to a polemic issued in form of a manifesto at Kilkenny by the high Irish ecclesiastics. In this Declaration, which is very curious reading, he exhorted the Irish to submit, and answered at great length the arguments of their religious leaders, with all the zeal, ingenuity, and acrimony of an eager theological disputant, and with an evident and burning sincerity to which many theological disputants do not attain. The religious side of his campaigns was always very strong in his mind, and no Puritan preacher more dearly loved setting forth the justification of his religious views, or answering the arguments of his religious opponents, whether Catholics or Covenanters.

So far as Puritanism was based upon a literal following of the example set in the Old Testament, it had a very dark, as well as a very exalted side. To take the inhuman butcheries of the early Jews as grateful to Jehovah, and therefore as justification for similar conduct by Christians, could lead only to deeds of horror. When Cromwell wrote from Cork, justifying the Puritan zeal which he admitted could not be justified by "reason if called before a jury," he appealed to the case of Phineas, who was held to have done the work of the Lord, because he thrust through the belly with his javelin the wretched Midianitish woman. No such plea can be admitted on behalf of peoples who have passed the stage of mere barbarism.

Drogheda and Wexford could not be excused by pointing out that the priests of the Jews of old had held it grateful to the Lord to kill without mercy the miserable women and children of the tribes whom the Israelites drove from the land. Such a position was in accord with the mediæval side of Cromwell's character, but was utterly out of touch with his thoroughly modern belief in justice and freedom for all men. Queer contradictions appear in the above-mentioned "Declaration," written, as he phrased it, "For the undeceiving of deluded and seduced people." He showed that he was a leader in the modern movement for social, political, and religious liberty, when he wrote: "Arbitrary power men begin to grow weary of, in Kings and Churchmen; their juggle between them mutually to uphold civil and ecclesiastical tyranny begins to be transparent. Some have cast off both; and hope by the Grace of God to keep so. Others are at it." But when he came to reconcile his own declarations for religious liberty with his previous refusal to permit the celebration of the mass, he was forced into a purely technical justification of his position. He announced that he would punish, with all the severity of the law, priests "seducing the people, or, by any overt act, violating the laws established," but added: "As for the people what thoughts they have in matters of religion in their own breasts, I cannot reach; but shall think it my duty, if they walk honestly and peaceably, not to cause them in the least to suffer for the same." In other words, Catholics could believe what they wished, but were not allowed to profess their beliefs in the form that they desired, or to have their teachers among them. To our American eyes such a position is so wholly untenable, so shocking to the moral sense, that it requires an effort to remember that it was in advance of the position taken in the next century by the English toward the Irish through their Penal Laws, and of the position taken in France toward the Protestants during the latter part of the reign of Louis XIV. and all the reign of Louis XV., while of course it was infinitely beyond the theory upon which the temporal and spiritual authorities of Spain acted.

While the Irish campaign was at its height, the Scotch, who had declared for Charles II., made ready for war, and the English Parliament demanded Cromwell's return. For some months, however, he remained in Ireland, capturing Kilkenny and various other towns and castles and constantly extending the area of English sway, driving the Irish westward. His campaign was a model for all military operations undertaken in a difficult country, covered by a network of fortified places, and held by masses of guerillas or irregular levies, backed by the whole population. After Clonmel was taken he handed over the command to Ireton; the heavy work had been done, and what remained to do was tedious and harassing rather than formidable, while the Scotch business could no longer wait.

In May, 1650, Cromwell landed in England, took his seat in the House of Commons, and was made Captain-General and Commander-in-Chief of the forces, Fairfax having refused to take part in any offensive campaign against the Covenanters. It is recorded that when Cromwell entered London, greeted by surging multitudes, someone called his attention to the way the people turned out to do him honor for his triumph; whereupon he dryly answered that it was nothing to the way they would turn out to see him hanged.

The refusal of Fairfax to march against the Scotch left Cromwell the only hope of the Commonwealth. It cannot too often be repeated that, whether in the end Cromwell's ambitions did or did not obscure the high principles with which they certainly blended, yet he rose to supreme power less by his own volition than by the irresistible march of events, and because he was "a man of the mighty days, and equal to the days." In this world, in the long run, the job must necessarily fall to the man who both can and will do it when it must be done, even though he does it roughly or imperfectly. It is well enough to deplore and to strive against the conditions which make it necessary to do the job; but when once face to face with it, the man who fails either in power or will, the man who is half-hearted, reluctant, or incompetent, must give way to the actual doer, and he must not complain because the doer gets the credit and reward. President Buchanan utterly disbelieved in the right of secession, but he also felt doubts as to its being constitutional or possible to "coerce a sovereign state," and therefore he and those who thought like him had to give place to men who felt no such doubts. It may be the highest duty to oppose a war before it is brought on, but once the country is at war, the man who fails to support it with all possible heartiness comes perilously near being a traitor, and his conduct can only be justified on grounds which in time of peace would justify a revolution. The whole strength of the English Commonwealth was in the Independents. Royalists, Episcopalians, Presbyterians, extreme Levellers, were all against it. When the Scotch declared for Charles II. as King, not only of Scotland but of England, they rendered it necessary that either England or Scotland should be conquered. Fairfax declared that he was willing to defend the English against the Scotch attack, but not to attack Scotland. The position was puerile; a fact which should be borne in mind by the excellent persons who at the present day believe that a nation can be somehow armed for defence without being armed for attack. No fight was ever yet won by parrying alone; hard hitting is the best parry; the offensive is the only sure defensive. To refuse to attack the Scotch was merely to give them a great initial advantage in the inevitable struggle. Cromwell was far too clear-sighted and resolute to suffer from oversentimental scruples in the matter. Accordingly he undertook the task; did it with his accustomed thoroughness; and from that moment became, not merely the first man in the Kingdom, but a man without a second or a third, without a rival of any kind.

Charles had landed in Scotland and been proclaimed King, but was forced not merely to take the Covenant but to make degrading professions of abandonment and renunciation of his father's acts and principles. He was, after all, to be a King only in name, if the dominant party in Scotland could have its way. Dour as Dopper Boers, the Covenanters were determined that the government should be, though in form royal, in essence a democratic theocracy, where the men of the strictest Calvinistic sect should all have their say in an administration marked by the most bitter intolerance of every religious belief which differed by even a shade from their own. To get real religious liberty in those days one had to go to Rhode Island or Maryland; but at least the English Puritans were, in this respect, far in advance of the men against whom they were pitted.

There was also a Royalist party in Scotland, which had scant sympathy with the Covenanters, but was only allowed to exist at all by their sufferance. When at this time Montrose landed to help the King, the Presbyterian friends of the King promptly overcame and slew him. The Kirk was supreme, and in the army which it gathered to meet Cromwell it made zeal for the Covenant the all-important requirement for a commission. It would not even permit places of command to be given to the officers who had marched with Hamilton's army. The Royalists around the King complained bitterly that the commissions were most apt to go to sons of ministers, and if not, then to men whose godliness and religious enthusiasm were but poor substitutes for training and skill in arms. Cromwell's soldiers possessed all of these qualities. Devotion to country or to religion adds immensely to the efficiency of a soldier, but is a broken reed by itself. Officers whose only qualifications are religious or patriotic zeal, are better than officers who seek service to gratify their vanity, or who are appointed through political favor; but until they have really learned their business, and unless they are eager and able to learn it, this is all that can be said of them.

Cromwell marched north to the walls of Edinburgh, where David Leslie lay with the Covenanting army of the Kirk. Leslie had fought under Gustavus Adolphus, and beside Cromwell at Marston Moor, where the Scotch insisted that they had saved the Cromwellians from defeat. Now the two sides were decisively to test the question of supremacy. But the contest was really utterly unequal. Cromwell had a veteran army, one which had been kept under arms for years. Leslie had an army which had been brought together for this particular war. He was, therefore, under the terrible disadvantage which rests on any man who, with raw volunteers, confronts well-trained, well-led veterans. There were under him plenty of officers and men with previous military experience—though, as the Royalist above quoted remarked, too many of the officers were "sanctified creatures who hardly ever saw or heard of any sword but that of the Spirit"—yet the regiments were all new, and the men had no regimental pride or confidence, no knowledge of how to act together, no trust in one another or in their commanders; while Cromwell's regiments were old, and the recruits in each at once took their tone from the veterans around them.

Although Leslie's force was twice that of Cromwell's, he knew his trade too well to risk a stricken field on equal terms, when the soldiers were of such unequal quality. He accordingly intrenched in a strong position covering Edinburgh, and there awaited the English attack. Cromwell was a born fighter, always anxious for the trial of the sword; a man who habitually took castles and walled towns by storm, himself at need heading the stormers, and who won his pitched battles by the shock of his terrible cavalry, which he often led in person, and which invariably ruined any foe whom he had overthrown. He now advanced with too much confidence and found himself in a very ugly situation; his men sickening rapidly, while Leslie's army increased in numbers and discipline. Like every great commander, Cromwell realized that the end of all manœuvring is to fight—that the end of strategy should be the crushing overthrow in battle of the enemy's forces. On this occasion his eagerness made him forget his caution; and all his masterly skill was needed to extricate him from the position into which he had been plunged by his own overbearing courage and the wariness of his opponent.

For some time he lay before Edinburgh, unable to get Leslie to fight, and of course unwilling to attack him in his intrenchments. Sickness and lack of provisions finally forced him to retreat. He believed that this would draw Leslie out of his works, and his belief was justified by the event. The English now mustered some 11,000 men; the Scotch, 22,000. Leslie was still cautious about fighting, but the ministers of the Kirk, who were with him in great numbers, hurried him on. He followed Cromwell to Dunbar, where he cut off the English retreat to England. But his army was on the hills and was suffering from the weather. He thought that the discouraged English were about to embark on their ships. The ministers fiercely urged him to destroy the "sectaries" whom they so hated, and in the afternoon of December 2d he crowded down toward the lower ground, near the sea.

Cromwell saw with stern joy that at last the Scotch had given him the longed-for chance, and true to his instincts he at once decided to attack, instead of waiting to be attacked. Leslie's troops had come down the steep slopes, and at their foot were crowded together so that their freedom of movement was much impaired. Cromwell believed that if their right wing were smashed, the left could not come in time to its support. He pointed this out to Lambert, who commanded his horse, and to Monk, the saturnine tobacco-chewing colonel, now a devoted and trusted Cromwellian. Both agreed with Cromwell, and before dawn the English army was formed for the onslaught, the officers and troopers praying and exhorting loudly. Their cry was: "The Lord of Hosts!" that of their Presbyterian foes: "The Covenant!" It was a strange fight, this between the Puritan and the Covenanter, whose likeness in the intensity of their religious zeal and in the great features of their creeds but embittered their antagonism over the smaller points upon which they differed.

Day dawned, while driving gusts of rain swept across the field, and the soldiers on both sides stood motionless. Then the trumpets sounded the charge, and the English horse, followed by the English foot, spurred against the stubborn Scottish infantry of Leslie's right wing. The masses of Scotch cavalry, with their lancers at the head, fell on the English horse—disordered by the contest with the infantry—and pushed them back into the brook; but they rallied in a moment, as the reserves came up, and horse and foot again rushed forward to the attack. At this moment the sun flamed red over the North Sea, and Cromwell shouted aloud, with stern exultation: "Let God arise and let His enemies be scattered," and a few moments later—"They run! I profess they run!" for now the Scottish army broke in wild confusion, though one brigade of foot held their ground, fighting the English infantry at push of pike and butt-end of musket, until a troop of the victorious horse charged from one end to the other, through and through them.

Cromwell was as terrible in pursuit as in battle. He never left a victory half-won, and always followed the fleeing foe, as Sheridan followed the Confederates before Appomattox. The English horse pressed the fleeing Scotch, and their defeat became the wildest rout, their cavalry riding through their infantry. Cromwell himself rallied and reformed his troopers, who sang as a song of praise the hundred and seventeenth Psalm; and then he again loosed his squadrons on the foe. The fight had not lasted an hour, and Cromwell's victory cost him very little; but of the Scotch, 3,000 were put to the sword, chiefly in the pursuit, and 10,000 were captured, with 30 guns and 200 colors. Leslie escaped by the speed of his horse. Never had Cromwell won a greater triumph. Like Jackson in his Valley Campaigns, though he was greatly outnumbered, he struck the foe at the decisive point with the numbers all in his own favor, and by taking advantage of their error he ruined them at a blow. Like most great generals, Cromwell's strategy was simple, and in the last resort consisted in forcing the enemy to fight on terms that rendered it possible thoroughly to defeat him; and like all great generals, he had an eye which enabled him to take advantage of the fleeting opportunities which occur in almost every battle, but which if not instantly grasped vanish forever.

The ruin of the Kirk brought to the front the Cavaliers, who still surrounded Charles and were resolute to continue the fight. Both before and after Dunbar, Cromwell carried on a very curious series of theological disputations with the leaders of the Kirk party. The letters and addresses of the two sides remind one of the times when Byzantine Emperors exchanged obscure theological taunts with the factions of the Circus. Yet this correspondence reveals no little of the secret of Cromwell's power; of his intense religious enthusiasm—which was both a strength and a weakness—his longing for orderly liberty, and his half-stifled aspirations for religious freedom.

He was on sound ground in his controversy with the Scottish Kirk. He put the argument for religious freedom well when he wrote to the Governor of Edinburgh Castle, concerning his ecclesiastical opponents: "They assume to be the infallible expositors of the Covenant (and of the Scriptures), counting a different sense and judgment from theirs Breach of Covenant and Heresy—no marvel they judge of others so authoritatively and severely. But we have not so learned Christ. We look at Ministers as helpers of, not Lords over, God's people. I appeal to their consciences whether any 'man' trying their doctrines and dissenting shall not incur the censure of Sectary? And what is this but to deny Christians their liberty and assume the Infallible Chair? What doth (the Pope) do more than this?"

There is profitable study for many people of to-day in the following: "Your pretended fear lest error should step in is like the man who would keep all the wine out of the country, lest men should be drunk. It will be found an unjust and unwise jealousy to deprive a man of his natural liberty upon a supposition he may abuse it. When he doth abuse it, judge. If a man speak foolishly, ye suffer him gladly, because ye are wise. Stop such a man's mouth by sound words which cannot be gainsayed. If he speak to the disturbance of the public peace, let the civil magistrate punish him."

After Dunbar, Cromwell could afford to indulge in such

disputations, for, as he said: "The Kirk had done their do." All that remained was to deal with the Cavaliers. There is, by the way, a delightful touch of the "Trust in the Lord, and keep your powder dry!" type in one of his letters of this time, when he desired the Commander at Newcastle to ship him three or four score masons, "for we expect that God will suddenly put some places into our hands which we shall have occasion to fortify."

The fate of the prisoners taken at Dunbar was dreadful. War had not learned any of its modern mercifulness. Cromwell was in this, as in other respects, ahead, and not behind, the times. He released half of the prisoners—for the most part half-starved, sick, and wounded—and sent the rest under convoy southward, praying that humanity might be exercised toward them; but no care was taken of them, and four-fifths died from starvation and pestilence.

Meanwhile, a new Scotch army was assembling at Stirling, consisting for the most part of the Lowland Cavaliers, with their retainers, and the Royalist chiefs from the Highlands, with their clansmen. Before acting against them, Cromwell broke up the remaining Kirk forces, put down the moss-troopers and plunderers, and secured the surrender of Edinburgh. Winter came on, and operations ceased during the severe weather.

In the spring of 1651, he resumed his work, and by the end of summer he had the Royalists in such plight that it was evident that their only chance was to abide the hazard of a great effort. Early in August Charles led his army across the border into England, to see if he could not retrieve his cause there, while Cromwell was in Scotland; but Cromwell himself promptly followed him, while Cromwell's lieutenants in England opposed and hampered the march of the Royalists. There was need of resolute action, for Charles had the best Scotch army that had yet been gathered together. There was no general rising of the English to join him, but, when he reached Worcester, the town received him with open arms. This was the end of his successes. Cromwell came up, and after careful preparation, delivered his attack, on September 3d. Charles had only some 15,000 men; Cromwell, nearly 30,000, half of whom, however, were the militia of the neighboring counties, who were not to be compared either with Cromwell's own veterans, or with their Royalist opponents. The fight was fierce, Cromwell's left wing gradually driving back the enemy, in spite of stubborn resistance; while, on his right, the Cavaliers and Highlanders themselves vigorously attacked the troops to which they were opposed. It was "as stiff a contest for four or five hours as ever I have seen," wrote Cromwell that evening; but at last he overthrew his foes, and, following them with his usual vigor, frightful carnage ensued. The victory was overwhelming. Charles himself escaped after various remarkable adventures, but all the nobles and generals of note were killed or taken. Nearly 11,000 men were captured, and practically all the remainder were slain.

This was, as Cromwell said, "the crowning mercy." It was the last fight of the Civil War; the last time that Cromwell had to lead an army in the field. From now till his death there never appeared in England a foe it was necessary for him to meet in person.

V. THE COMMONWEALTH AND PROTECTORATE

After the battle of Worcester, the authority of the Commonwealth was supreme throughout the British Islands. This authority as yet reposed, wholly in form, largely in substance, with the remnant of the Long Parliament. This remnant, derisively called the "rump," differed as widely in power and capacity from the Parliament led by Pym and Hampden, as the Continental Congress that saw the outgoing of the Revolutionary War differed from that which saw its incoming. Defections and purgings, exclusions first of whole-hearted Episcopalian Royalists and then of half-hearted Presbyterian Royalists, had reduced it to being but the representative of a faction. It had submitted to the supremacy of the army by submitting to the exclusion of those members to whom the army objected. Then it had worked for some time hand in hand with the army; but, now that war was over, the Parliamentary representatives or the Independents feared more and more the supremacy of the military, or Cromwellian, wing of their party. It was the army, and not the Parliament, that had won the fight; that had killed one king, and driven another, his son, into exile; that had subdued Scotland and Ireland, and stamped out the last vestige of Royalist resistance in England. Yet it was the Parliament, and not the army, which in theory was to fall heir to the royal power.

Moreover, Parliament, thanks to its past history, had become as little as the army the legal embodiment of the power of England; and what was more important, there was even less general acceptance of it as the proper representative of power, than there was general acceptance of the army. The army, even where hated, was feared and respected; the Parliament was beginning to excite no emotion save an angry contempt. There were men of honor, of note, and of ability still left in the Parliament; but its vital force was dying.

Conscious of its own weakness before the people, the Parliament was most reluctant to face a dissolution; most eager to devise means by which its rule could be perpetuated. The army, no less conscious of the hostility felt for it by the Parliament, was just as determined that there should be a dissolution and an election of a new Parliament. In the approaching conflict the army had an immense advantage, for, while the Parliament was losing its grip upon the Independents, without in any way attracting strength from the Royalists, the great mass of the Independents still firmly regarded Cromwell as their especial champion.

This was the case, not only in England, but elsewhere. One of Cromwell's letters of about this time is to the New England clergyman, John Cotton, in answer to one which showed the keen interest taken in Cromwell's triumph by his fellow-Puritans, who, across the Atlantic, had begun the upbuilding of what is now the giant republic of the New World. The letter is marked by the continuous use of scriptural phrases and protestations of humility, so ostentatious and overstrained as to convey an uncomfortable feeling of hypocrisy; yet, without doubt, there was a base of genuineness for these expressions. Beyond question, Cromwell felt that he was doing the Lord's work; and was sustained through the tremendous hours of labor and peril by the sense of battling for justice on this earth, and in accordance with the Eternal Will of Heaven.

In dealing with Cromwell and the Puritan Revolution it must ever be kept in mind, before judging too harshly the actors, that the era saw the overlapping of two systems, both in religion and in politics; and many incongruities resulted. It was the first great stride toward the practical achievement of civil rights and individual liberty as we now understand them. It was also the era in which the old theological theory of the all-importance of dogma came into sharp conflict with the now healthily general religious belief in the superior importance of conduct. Of course, as is invariably the case in real life, the issues were not sharply drawn at all points, and at some they were wholly obscured by the strong passions and ambitions which belong, not to any particular age, but to all time.

After Worcester, when Cromwell had returned to London, he one day summoned a conference, at Speaker Lenthall's house, of the leaders of the Parliamentary army to decide how the national destiny was to be settled. He hoped that they would be able to form a policy among themselves; but the hope proved fruitless. Some of the members wished an absolute republic; some wished a setting-up of what we would now call a limited monarchy, with one of the late king's sons recalled and put at the head.

Nothing came of the conference, and Parliament went its way. It had at last waked to the fact that it must do something positive in the way of reform, or else that its days were numbered. It began with great reluctance to make a pretence of preparing for its own dissolution, and strove to accomplish some kind of reform in the laws. At that time the law of England had been for generations little more than a mass of ingenious technicalities, and the Court of Chancery had become the synonym for a system of interminable delay, which worked as much injustice as outright spoliation. Even now there is a tendency in the law toward the deification of technicalities, the substitution of the letter for the spirit; a tendency which can only be offset by a Bench, and, indeed, a Bar, possessing both courage and common-sense. At that time, the condition of affairs was much worse, and the best men in England shared the popular feeling of extreme dislike for lawyers, as men whose trade was not to secure justice, but to weave a great web of technicalities which completely defeated justice. However, reform in the methods of legal procedure proved as difficult then as it ever has proved, and all that even Cromwell could do was to make a beginning in the right direction. The Rump was quite unable so much as to make this beginning.

The Parliament obtained a momentary respite by creating a diversion in foreign affairs, and bringing on a war with the Dutch. Throughout the first half of the seventeenth century, the Dutch were the leading mercantile and naval power of Europe, surpassing the English in trade and in colonial possessions. Unfortunately for them, their home authorities did not believe in preparedness for war; and the crushing defeats which the boldness and skill of their sailors had enabled them to inflict on the Spaniards, lulled them into the unwholesome faith—shared at times by great modern mercantile communities—that, by simple desire for peace, they could avert war; and that if war came, they could trust to their riches and reserve strength to win. Accordingly, in time of peace they laid up their warships and never built a fighting navy in advance, trusting to the use of armed merchant-vessels and improvised war-craft to meet the need of the hour. England, on the contrary, had a large regular navy, the ships being superior in size and armament to the Dutch, and the personnel of the navy being better disciplined, although none of the English Admirals, save Blake, ranked with Tromp and De Ruyter.

The cause of the quarrel was the Navigation Act, passed by England for the express purpose of building up the English commercial marine at the expense of the Dutch. The latter were then the world's carriers on the ocean. They derived an immense profit from carrying the goods of other countries, in their own bottoms, from these other countries to England. The Navigation Act forbade this, allowing only English bottoms to be used to carry goods to England, unless the goods were carried in the ships of the country from which they came. This is the kind of measure especially condemned by the laissez-faire school of economists, and its good results in this case have always puzzled them; while, on the other hand, its success under one set of conditions has been often ignorantly held to justify its application under entirely different conditions. In other words, like the system of protective tariffs, it is one of those economic measures which may or may not be useful to a country, according to changes in time and circumstances. In the Cromwellian period it benefited the English as much as it hurt the Dutch, and laid the foundation of English commercial supremacy. Another cause of war was the insistance by the English upon their right to have their flag saluted by the Dutch as well as by other foreign powers.

There followed a bloody and obstinate struggle for the mastery of the seas. Battle after battle was fought between the Dutch and English fleets. The latter were commanded by Blake, Monk,

Dean, and other officers, who had won distinction ashore—for the process of differentiation between military service on land and on the sea was far from complete. The fighting was most determined, and the Dutch won two or three victories; but they were defeated again and again, until finally beaten into submission. The war was one undertaken purely from motives of commercial greed, against the nation which, among all the nations of continental Europe, stood closest to England in religious belief, in form of government, in social ideas, and in its system of political liberty. Cromwell hated the thought of the two free Protestant powers battling one another to exhaustion, while every ecclesiastical and political tyranny looked on with a grin of approbation. He wished the alliance, not the enmity, of Holland; and though, when the war was once on, he and those he represented refused in any way to embarrass their own government, yet they were anxious for peace. The Parliament, on the other hand, hailed the rise of the Navy under Blake as a counterpoise to the power of the army under Cromwell. One effect of this Dutch War was to postpone the question of the dissolution of Parliament; another, to cause increased taxation, which was met by levying on the estates of the Royalist Delinquents, so-called.

By March, 1653, the Dutch were evidently beaten, and peace was in sight; but before peace came, there was an end of the Rump Parliament. The discontent in the army had steadily increased. They wished a thorough reform in governmental methods; and with the characteristic Puritan habit of thought, wished especially to guarantee the safety of the "Godly interests" by a complete new election. On the other hand, the Parliament was scheming how to yield in name only, and not in fact, and had hit on the device of passing a bill which should continue all the members of the existing Parliament without reëlection; and, moreover, should constitute them a general committee, with full power to pass upon the qualifications of any new members elected. This, of course, amounted to nothing, and the army would not accept it.

Many conferences of the leaders of the two sides were held at Cromwell's house, the last on the evening of April 19, 1653, young Sir Harry Vane, formerly one of Cromwell's close friends, being among the number of the Parliamentary leaders. Cromwell, on behalf of his party, warned them that their bill could not be accepted or submitted to, and the Parliamentary leaders finally agreed that it should not be brought up again in the House, until after further conference. But they either did not or could not keep their agreement. The members of the House were obstinately resolved to keep their places—many of them from corrupt motives, for they had undoubtedly made much money out of their positions, through the taxing of delinquents and otherwise. In short, they wished to perpetuate their government, to have England ruled by a little self-perpetuating oligarchy. Next morning, April 20th, Parliament met and the leaders began to hurry the Bill through the House.

They reckoned without their host. Cromwell, sitting in his reception-room, and waiting the return of the conferees of last evening, learned what was going on, and just as he was clad, "in plain black clothes and gray worsted stockings," followed by a few officers and twenty or thirty stark musketeers, he walked down to the House. There he sat and listened for some time to the debate on the Bill, once beckoning over Harrison, the Republican general, his devoted follower. When the question was put as to whether the Bill should pass, he rose and broke in with one of his characteristic speeches. First, he enumerated the good that had been done by Parliament, and then began to tell them of their injustice, their heed to their own self-interests, their delay to do right. One among his eager listeners called him to order, but no appeal to Parliamentary forms could save the doomed House. "Come, come!" answered Oliver, "we have had enough of this; I will put an end to your prating!" With that he clapped on his hat, stamped on the floor with his feet, and began to rate the Commons as if they were disobedient school-boys. "It is not fit that you should sit here any longer; you have sat too long for any good that you have been doing lately; you shall now give place to better men!" And Harrison called in the musketeers. Oliver then continued, enumerating the sins of the members, some of whom were drunkards, some lewd livers, some corrupt and unjust. The house was on its feet as he lifted the mace, saying: "What shall we do with this bauble? Take it away!" and gave it to a musketeer; and then, turning toward the Speaker: "Fetch him down!" and fetched down he was. Gloomily the members went out, while Cromwell taunted Sir Harry Vane with breaking his promise, ending with: "The Lord deliver me from thee, Sir Harry Vane!" So ended the Long Parliament and, asserted Oliver, "We did not hear a dog bark at their going."

Tomes have been written to prove whether Oliver was right or wrong in what he did at this time; but the Rump Parliament had no claim to be, either in law or fact, the representative of the English people, or of any part of them that really counted. There was no justification for its continuance, and no good whatever could come from permitting it to exist longer. Its actions, and especially its obstinate determination to perpetuate its own rule, without warrant in law, without the even higher and more perilous warrant of justice and national need, rendered it necessary that it should be dissolved. At the time Cromwell, without doubt, intended that it should be replaced by a genuinely representative body; and if he had possessed the temper, the self-control, the far-sighted patriotism, and the personal disinterestedness which would have enabled him to carry out his intentions in good faith, without thinking of his own interests, he would have rendered an inestimable public service and might have advanced by generations the movement for English liberty.

In other words, if Cromwell had been a Washington, the Puritan Revolution might have been made permanent. His early acts, after the dissolution of the Long Parliament, showed a sincere desire on his part, and on the part of those whose leader he was, to provide some form of government which should secure justice and order, without leaving everything to the will of one man. His first effort was to summon an assembly of the Puritan notables. In the interim he appointed a new Council of State, with himself, as Captain-General, at its head. The fleet, the army, and the Independents generally, all hastened to pledge him their support, and England undoubtedly acquiesced in his action, being chiefly anxious to see whether or not the new Assembly could formulate a permanent scheme of government. If the Assembly and Cromwell together could have done this—that is, could have done work like that of the great Convention which promulgated the Constitution of the United States—all would have gone well.

In criticising Cromwell, however, we must remember that generally in such cases an even greater share of blame must attach to the nation than to the man. Free government is only for nations that deserve it; and they lose all right to it by licentiousness, no less than by servility. If a nation cannot govern itself, it makes comparatively little difference whether its inability springs from a slavish and craven distrust of its own powers, or from sheer incapacity on the part of its citizens to exercise self-control and to act together. Self-governing freemen must have the power to accept necessary compromises, to make necessary concessions, each sacrificing somewhat of prejudice, and even of principle, and every group must show the necessary subordination of its particular interests to the interests of the community as a whole. When the people will not or cannot work together; when they permit groups of extremists to decline to accept anything that does not coincide with their own extreme views; or when they let power slip from their hands through sheer supine indifference; then they have themselves chiefly to blame if the power is grasped by stronger hands. Yet, while keeping all this in mind, it must not be forgotten that a great and patriotic leader may, if the people have any capacity for self-government whatever, help them upwards along their hard path by his wise leadership, his wise yielding to even what he does not like, and his wise refusal to consider his own selfish interests. A people thoroughly unfit for self-government, as were the French at the end of the eighteenth century, are the natural prey of a conscienceless tyrant like Napoleon. A people like the Americans of the same generation can be led along the path of liberty and order by a Washington. The English people, in the middle of the seventeenth century, might have been helped to entire self-government by Cromwell, but were not sufficiently advanced politically to keep him from making himself their absolute master if he proved morally unequal to rising to the Washington level; though doubtless they would not have tolerated a man of the Napoleonic type.

The Assembly gathered in July, 1653. It was called the "Barebones" Parliament in derision, because one of its members—a Puritan leather-merchant—was named "Praise-God Barbon." The members were men of high character, of intense religious fervor, and, for the most part, of good social standing. They were actuated by sincere conviction, but they had no political training whatever. They were not accustomed to make government move; they were theorists, rather than doers. Religious fervor, or mere fervor for excellence in the abstract, is a great mainspring for good work in politics as in war, but it is no substitute for training, in either civil or military life; and if not accompanied by sound common-sense and a spirit of broad tolerance, it may do as much damage as any other mighty force which is unregulated.

On July 4th, Cromwell opened the Assembly with a long speech, which, toward the end, became a true Puritan sermon; a speech which had in it a very high note of religion and morality, but which showed a growing tendency in Oliver's mind to appeal from the judgment of men to what he esteemed the judgment of Heaven, whenever he thought men were wrong. Now, it is very essential that a man should have in him the capacity to defy his fellows if he thinks that they are doing the work of the Devil, and not the work of the Lord; but it is even more essential for him to remember that he must be most cautious about mistaking his own views for those of the Lord; and also to remember that as the Lord's work is accomplished through human instruments, and as these can only be used to advantage by remembering that they are human, and, therefore, imperfect, in the long run a man can do nothing of permanence, save by joining his zeal to sound judgment, moderation, and the desire to accomplish practical results.

The Assembly of Puritan notables was no more competent to initiate successful self-government in England than a Congress of Abolitionists, in 1860, would have been competent to govern the

United States. They did not lack in lofty devotion to their ideals, but their methods were impractical. Cromwell professed to have resigned his power into their hands, and they went at their work in a spirit of high religious enthusiasm. The "instrument," under which they were summoned, had provided that their authority should be transferred to another assembly elected under their directions; in other words, they were to form a constitutional Convention. They undertook a host of reforms, largely in the right direction. Among other things, they proposed the abolition of the Court of Chancery, the establishment of civil marriage, the abolition of tithes, and of lay patronage. The clergy and the lawyers were cast into a frenzy of alarm over these proposals, and the landed proprietors became very uneasy lest some of their own unjust vested interests should suffer.

Now, all this was most excellent in point of moral purpose, just as it would have been absolutely right, from the abstract ethical stand-point, if the Constitution of 1789, or the Republican Convention of 1860, had declared for the abolition of slavery in all the States. Of course, if the Constitution had made such a declaration, it would never have been adopted, and the English-speaking people of North America would have plunged into a condition of anarchy like that of the after-time South American Republics; while, if the Republican platform of 1860 had taken such a position, Lincoln would not have been elected, no war for the Union would have been waged, and instead of slavery being abolished, it would have been perpetuated in at least one of the confederacies into which the country would have been split. The Barebones Parliament was too far ahead of the times, too indifferent to results, and too impatient of the limitations and prejudices of its neighbors. Its members were reformers, who lost sight of the fact that a reform must be practicable in order to make it of value. They excited the utmost suspicion in the community at large, and Cromwell, whose mind was in many respects very conservative, and who was an administrator rather than a constructive statesman, shared the general uneasiness. He shrank from the acts of the Barebones Parliament just as he had shrunk from the levelling tendencies of the Republicans. The leaders of both had gone too far in the direction of speculative reform. Cromwell erred on the other side, and did not go far enough. It is just as necessary for the practical man to remember that his practical qualities are useless, or worse than useless, unless he joins with them that spirit of striving after better things which marks the reformer, as it is for this same reformer to remember that he cannot give effective expression to his desire for a higher life save by following rigidly practical ways.

Cromwell, in his opening address to the Convention, had been carried away by his religious enthusiasm, and in a burst of strange, rugged eloquence had bid his hearers remember that they must "hold themselves accountable to God only;" must own their call to be from Him, and must strive to bring about God's rule upon earth. When they took his words literally he became heartily uneasy, as did the great bulk of Englishmen; for, of course, there were limitless interpretations to be put as to the proper way of being "owned" by God, and Oliver was not in the least inclined to accept the interpretation adopted by the Barebones Parliament. He wished administrative reform in Church and State, but he had little sympathy with what he deemed revolutionary theories, whether good or bad.

The Convention gradually grew conscious that it had no support in popular sympathy, and dissolved of its own motion, after having named a Council of State, which drew up a remarkable Constitution under the name of the "Instrument of Government." This Instrument was adopted by Cromwell and the Council of Officers, and under it a new Parliament was convened. Even yet, Cromwell, and at least the majority of the army, shrank from abandoning every effort at constitutional rule in favor of the naked power of the sword. Nevertheless, Cromwell had even less fondness for the rule of a Parliament elected under any conditions he was able to devise. He realized that the majority of the nation was against him, and dreaded lest it might take steps toward the rehabilitation of the monarchy. In his address to the Barebones Convention he had dwelt with special emphasis upon the fact that a Parliament elected merely by the majority might not be nearly so suitable for doing the Lord's work as such an assembly as that he had convened.

In short, all his qualities, both good and bad, tended to render the forms and the narrowly limited powers of constitutional government irksome to him. His strength, his intensity of conviction, his delight in exercising powers for what he conceived to be good ends; his dislike of speculative reforms and his inability to appreciate the necessity of theories to a practical man who wishes to do good work; his hatred of both King and oligarchy, while he utterly distrusted a popular majority; his tendency to insist upon the superiority of the moral law, as he saw it, to the laws of mankind round about him—all these tendencies worked together to unfit him for the task of helping a liberty-loving people on the road toward freedom.

The Instrument of Government was a very remarkable document. It was a written constitution. Cromwell and his soldiers desired, like Washington and his fellow-members of the Constitutional Convention which framed the government of the United States, to have the fundamental law of the land put in shape where it would be accessible to all men, and where its terms would not be open to doubt. Such a course was absolutely necessary if a free government, in the modern sense, was to be established on radically new lines. It has not been rendered necessary in the free England of to-day, because, very fortunately, England has been able to reach her freedom by evolution, not revolution.

The Instrument of Government confided the executive power to a Lord Protector and Council; Cromwell was named as the first Protector. The legislative power was assigned without restriction to a Parliament elected by constituencies formed on a new and equitable franchise, there being a sweeping redistribution of seats. Parliament could pass a Bill over the Protector's veto, and was to meet once in three years, for at least five months; but it had little control over the executive, save that with it rested the initiative in filling vacancies in the Council. The Protector was allotted a certain fixed sum, which made him largely independent of the Parliament's action. Nevertheless, the Protector was under real constitutional control. Religious liberty was secured for all congregations which did not admit "papacy or prelacy," the Episcopalians and Roman Catholics being excluded from this right just as they were excluded from the right of voting, rather as enemies to the Commonwealth than because of their mere religious beliefs. They were regarded as what would now be called, in the political terminology of continental Europe, "irreconcilables"; and the mass and the Prayer-Book were both prohibited. Until the first Parliament met, which was to be on the anniversary of the Battle of Dunbar, on September 3d, 1654, the Protector and Council were to issue ordinances with the force of law.

The Constitution thus had very many points of difference from that under which the United States grew into a great nation. Yet it ranks with it, rather than with the system of Parliamentary supremacy which was ultimately adopted in England. It was, of course, less popular, in the true sense, than the government of either the United States or Great Britain at the present moment. Oliver, later on, insisted on what he called the "Four Fundamentals," which answered to what we now style Constitutional Rights. His position was strictly in accord with the American, as opposed to the English, theory of embodying, by preference in some written document, propositions which neither the law-making body nor the executive could modify. It was not to be expected that he should hit on the device of a Supreme Court to keep guard over these propositions.

On December 16, 1653, Oliver was installed at Westminster, as Lord Protector. The judges, the army, the fleet, the mass of Independents, and the bulk of well-to-do citizens, concurred in the new departure; for the Protectorship gave stability, and the election of the new Parliament the assurance of liberty. There were plenty of opponents, however. The Royalists were implacable. The exiled House of Stuart, with a baseness of which their great opponent was entirely incapable, sought to compass his assassination. They could in no other way hope to reach the man whom they dared not look in the face on the field of battle. Plot after plot was formed to kill the Protector, but the plotters were invariably discovered and brought to justice; while every attempt at open insurrection was stamped out with the utmost ease. To the Royalist malcontents were added the extreme fanatics, the ultra-reformers of every type—religious, political, and social. These were, at the time, more dangerous than the Royalists, for they numbered supporters in the army, including some who had been prominent friends of Cromwell up to this time, like General Harrison. It was necessary, therefore, to arrest some of the most turbulent agitators, including preachers, and to deprive certain officers of their commissions.

The Protector and his Council acted wisely in their ordinances, redressing in practical shape many grievances. The Barebones Parliament had striven to abolish the Court of Chancery outright, and to hand its power over to the judges of the Common Law, which would merely have aggravated the existing hardships by checking the growth of the principle of equity. Oliver acted more conservatively: in fact, altogether too conservatively; but still he did something. In the Church government, also, a good deal was accomplished by the appointment of commissioners of good character to supervise the ministers, while allowing each to organize his congregation on any lines he chose—Presbyterian, Congregationalist, or Baptist. Dissenters were permitted to form separate congregations—"gathered churches" in the phrase of the day—if they so desired. Of course, this was not by any means complete religious toleration, but it was a nearer approach to it than any government in Europe, with the possible exception of the Dutch, had yet sanctioned, and it was so far in advance of the general spirit of the time that the new Parliament—a really representative body—took sharp exception to it. In point of religious toleration Oliver went just as far as the people of his day would let him—farther than any other ruler of the century was willing to go, save only Henry IV. of France—and Henry IV. really believed in nothing, and so could easily be tolerant, while Cromwell's zealous faith was part of the very marrow of his being.

Cromwell also concluded peace with the Dutch. Before the Long Parliament was dissolved it had become evident that the navy would ultimately conquer this peace for England; but the stubborn Dutch had to undergo several additional defeats before they would come to terms. Blake, the great admiral, had no particular admiration for Cromwell, but finally threw in his lot with him on the ground that the fleet had no concern with politics, and should limit itself strictly to the effort "to keep foreigners from fooling us." Monk was the admiral most in view in the later stages of the Dutch War. When it was over, he was sent back to keep the Highlands in order, which he and his fellow-Cromwellians did, with a thoroughness not afterward approached for a century. Scotland was now definitely united to England.

The new Parliament consisted of 400 members from England, 30 from Scotland, and 30 from Ireland. They were elected by a general suffrage, based on the possession of property to the value £200. The Parliament thus gathered was representative in a very wide sense. Nearly two hundred years were to elapse before any other as truly representative was to sit in England. The classes whose inclusion would certainly have made trouble were excluded; and, while the suffrage had been extended, and gross inequalities of representation abolished, there had been no such revolutionary action as suddenly to introduce masses of men unaccustomed to the exercise of self-government. Indeed, the house had arbitrarily erased from its roll of membership the names of a few ultra-Republicans. It was chiefly Cromwell's own fault that he failed to get along with this Parliament, and, therefore, failed to put the government on a permanent basis of orderly liberty.

At the beginning, everything seemed to go well. He opened the Parliament with one of those noteworthy speeches of which some seventeen have been preserved; speeches in the proper sense, unquestionably better when spoken to listeners than when read by critics, but instinct with the rough power of the speaker, permeated with religious fervor and sincere striving after the right; and even where the reasoning is most wrong-headed, containing phrases and sentiments which show the keenest insight into the needs of the moment, and the needs of eternity as well. The sentences are often very involved, it being quite evident that the speeches were not written out, not even deliberately thought out, in advance; for Oliver, even as he spoke, kept dropping and rejecting such of his half-finished utterances as did not give sufficiently accurate or vehement expression to his thought. Yet they contain abundance of the loftiest thought, expressed in language which merely gains strength from its rude, vigorous homeliness. For generations after Cromwell's death, the polished cynics and dull pedants, who abhorred and misunderstood him, spoke of his utterances with mixed ridicule and wrath: Hume hazarding the opinion that if his speeches, letters, and writings, were gathered together they would form "one of the most nonsensical collections the world had ever seen." We could far better afford to lose every line Hume ever wrote than the speeches of Cromwell.

In his opening address he pointed out that what the nation most needed was healing and settling; and in a spirit of thoroughly English conservatism, denounced any merely revolutionary doctrines which would do away with the security of property, or would give the tenant "as liberal a fortune" as the landlord. In religious matters also, he condemned those who could do nothing but cry: "Overturn! Overturn!! Overturn!!!" and together with his praise of what had been done, and of the body to which he spoke, he mingled much advice, remarking: "I hope you will not be unwilling to hear a little again of the sharp as well as of the sweet." He exhorted them to go to work in sober earnest; to remedy in practical shape any wrongs, and to join with him in working for good government. Unfortunately, he made the mental reservation that he should be himself the ultimate judge of what good government was.

Equally unfortunately, there was in the House a body of vehement Republicans who at once denied the legal existence of either Council or Protector, on the ground that the Long Parliament had never been dissolved. Of course such an argument was self-destructive, as it told equally against the legality of the new Parliament in which they sat. Parliament contented itself with recognizing the Instrument of Government as only of provisional validity, and proceeded to discuss it, clause by clause, as the groundwork of a new Constitution. It was unanimously agreed that Cromwell should retain his power for five years, but Parliament showed by its actions that it did not intend to leave him in a position of absolute supremacy. Instantly Oliver interfered, as arbitrarily as any hereditary King might have done.

He first appeared before the Parliament, and in an exceedingly able speech announced his willingness to accept a Parliamentary constitution, provided that it contained four fundamentals not to be overturned by law. The fundamentals were, first, that the country was to be governed by a single person, by a single executive, and a Parliament; second, that Parliaments were not to make themselves perpetual; third, that liberty of conscience should be respected; fourth, that the Protector and Parliament should have joint power over the militia.

All four propositions were sound. The first two were agreed to at once, and the third also, though with some reluctance, the Parliament being less liberal than the Protector in religious matters. Over the control of the soldiers there was irreconcilable difference.

Cromwell was not content with arguments. He would not permit any member to enter the House without signing an engagement not to alter the government as it had been settled; that is, every member had to subscribe to the joint government of the Protector and the Parliament. A hundred members refused to sign. Three-fourths of the House did sign, and went on with their work.

Until the assembling of this Parliament, every step that Oliver had taken could be thoroughly justified. He had not played the part of a usurper. He had been a zealous patriot, working in the interests of the people; and he had only broken up the Long Parliament when the Long Parliament had itself become an utterly unrepresentative body. He had then shown his good faith by promptly summoning a genuinely representative body. It is possible to defend him even for excluding the hundred members who declined to subscribe to his theory of the fundamentals of government. But it is not possible to excuse him for what he now did. Parliament, as it was left after the Extremists had been expelled, stood as the only elective body which it was possible to gather in England that could in any sense be called representative, and yet agree to work with Cromwell. Had Cromwell not become cursed with the love of power; had he not acquired a dictatorial habit of mind, and the fatal incapacity to acknowledge that there might be righteousness in other methods than his own, he could certainly have avoided a break with this Parliament. His splitting with it was absolutely needless. It agreed to confirm his powers for five years, and, as it happened, at the end of that time he was dead. Even had he lived there could be no possible excuse for refusing such a lease of power, on the ground that it was too short; for it was amply long enough to allow him to settle whatever was necessary to settle.

Cromwell, and later his apologists, insisted that, by delay and by refusing to grant supplies until their grievances were considered, the Parliament was encouraging the spirit of revolt. In reality the spirit of revolt was tenfold increased, not by the Parliament's action, but by Cromwell's, in seizing arbitrary power. If he had shown a tenth of the forbearance that Washington showed in dealing with the various Continental Congresses, he would have been readily granted far more power than ever Washington was given. He could easily have settled affairs on a constitutional basis, which would have given him all the power he had any right to ask; for his difficulties in this particular crisis were nothing like so great as those which Washington surmounted. The plea that the safety of the people and of the cause of righteousness depended upon his unchecked control, is a plea always made in such cases, and generally, as in this particular case, without any basis in fact. The need was just the other way.

Contrast Cromwell's conduct with that of Lincoln, just before his second election as President. There was a time in the summer of 1864 when it looked as if the Democrats would win, and elect McClellan. At that time it was infinitely more essential to the salvation of the Union that Lincoln should be continued in power, than it was to the salvation of the Commonwealth, in 1654, that Cromwell should be continued in power. Lincoln would have been far more excusable than Cromwell if he had insisted upon keeping control. Yet such a thought never entered Lincoln's head. He prepared to abide in good faith the decision of the people, and one of the most touching incidents of his life is the quiet and noble sincerity with which he made preparations, if McClellan was elected, to advise with him and help him in every way, and to use his own power, during the interval between McClellan's election and inauguration, in such a manner as would redound most to the advantage of the latter, and would increase, as far as possible, the chance for the preservation of the Union. It was at this time of Cromwell's life that, at the parting of the ways, he chose the wrong way. Great man though he was, and far though the good that he did out-balanced the evil, yet he lost the right to stand with men like Washington and Lincoln of modern times, and with the very, very few who, like Timoleon, in some measure approached their standard in ancient times.

As the Parliament continued in session, the attitude of the Protector changed from sullen to fierce hostility. It was entitled to sit five months. By a quibble he construed this to mean five lunar months. On January 22, 1655, he dissolved it, after rating it in a long and angry speech. With its dissolution it became evident to the great mass of true liberty-lovers that all hope of real freedom was at an end, and the forces that told for the restoration of the King were increased tenfold in strength. Nevertheless, some of the purest and most ardent lovers of liberty, like Milton, still clung despairingly to the Protector. They recognized that, with all his faults, and in spite of his determination to rule in arbitrary fashion, he yet intended to secure peace, justice, and good government, and, alike in power and in moral grandeur, towered above his only possible alternative, Charles II., as a giant towers above a pigmy.

VI. PERSONAL RULE

When Cromwell, in January, 1655, dismissed the first Protectorate Parliament, he left himself nothing to do but to establish his own personal rule; in other words, he became a tyrant. Of course the word cannot be used in the sense we use it in describing Ivan the Terrible, or Agathokles. As each country must, sooner or later, obtain exactly that measure of political freedom to which it is entitled, so, when it falls under a tyranny, the tyranny must be strictly conditioned by the character of the people. Cromwell ruled over Englishmen, not Russians or Greeks, and no Englishman would have tolerated for twenty-four hours what was groaningly borne by Muscovites, who had lost every vestige of manhood beneath the Tartar yoke, or by Syracusans, in the days of the rapid decadence of the Hellenistic world. Cromwell's government was a tyranny because it was based on his own personal rule, his personal decision as to what taxes should be levied, what ordinances issued, what police measures decreed and carried out, what foreign policy adopted or rejected. He was influenced very much by public opinion, when public opinion found definite expression in the action of a body of legislators or of an assembly of officers; but even in such cases he was only influenced, not controlled. In other words, he had gone back to the theory of government professed by the man he had executed, and by that man's predecessors. There was, however, the tremendous and far-reaching difference, that, whereas the Stuart kings clung to absolute power for the sake of rewarding favorites and of carrying out policies that were hostile to the honor and interest of England, Cromwell seized it with the sincere purpose of exalting the moral law at home and increasing the honor of England's name abroad. Moreover, he was in fact what no Stuart was, in anything but name: a "king among men," and his mighty strength enabled him, at least partially, to realize his purpose.

Cromwell doubtless persuaded himself that he was endeavoring to secure what would now be called a constitutional government: one which, in his own words, "should avoid alike the extremes of monarchy and democracy." He was desirous of paying heed to the wishes of those whom he esteemed the wisest and most honest among the people. He had somewhat of that gift for personal popularity which was so marked a feature of Queen Elizabeth—seemingly the only sovereign whom he admired, among all his predecessors. To the last he kept stirring vaguely for a constitutional system; and he sincerely disliked merely arbitrary rule.

But by the time he became Lord Protector he was too impatient of difference of opinion, too doggedly convinced of his own righteousness and wisdom, to be really fit to carry on a free government. He had sought to introduce the reign of the saints; but when, in the Barebones Parliament, he gathered together the very men whom he deemed their arch-representatives, it was only to find, as was of course inevitable, that he and they could not agree as to the method of realizing the reign of the saints in this very material world. Then he sought to secure a government by the representatives of the people: only to find that he got along even less well with them than with the saints. In short, while he had kept his nobility of purpose, his whole character had grown less and less such as to fit him to found a government of the kind toward which his race was dimly striving.

He made varied experiments for the control of England. After the first Protectorate Parliament had been abolished, he established the government of the major-generals, or in other words, purely military rule; dividing England into a dozen districts, with a major-general over each as the ultimate authority. The prime function of the major-generals was to keep order, and they crushed under their iron heels every spark of Royalist insurrection, or of Leveller and Anabaptist uprising. They interfered in civil matters also, and were especially required to see to the rigid observance of the Sabbath, and to suppress all cock-fighting, horse-racing, and kindred sports, as well as to shut up doubtful ale-houses. There certainly never was a more extraordinary despotism than this; the despotism of a man who sought power, not to gratify himself, or those belonging to him, in any of the methods to which all other tyrants have been prone; but to establish the reign of the Lord, as he saw it. Here was a tyrant who used the overwhelming strength of his military force to forbid what he considered profane amusements, and to enforce on one day of the week a system of conduct which was old-Jewish in character. Of course the fact that he meant well, and that his motives were high, did not make it any the easier for the people with whose pleasures and prejudices he thus irritatingly interfered.

The Puritan passion for regulating, not merely the religion, but the morals and manners of their neighbors, especially in the matter of Sunday observance and of pastimes generally, was peculiarly exasperating to men of a more easy-going nature. Even nowadays, the effort for practical reform in American city government is rendered immeasurably more difficult by the fact that a considerable number of the best citizens are prone to devote their utmost energies, not to striving for the fundamentals of social morality, civic honesty, and good government, but, in accordance with their own theory of propriety of conduct, to preventing other men from pursuing what these latter regard as innocent pleasures; while, on the other hand, a large number of good citizens, in their irritation at any interference with what they feel to be legitimate pastimes, welcome the grossest corruption and misrule rather than submit to what they call "Puritanism." When this happens, before our eyes, we need not wonder that in Cromwell's day the determination of the Puritans to put down ale-houses and prohibit every type of Sunday pastime, irritated large bodies of the people to the point of longing for the restoration of the Stuarts, no matter what might be the accompanying evils of corruption and tyranny.

The experiment of governing by the major-generals provoked such mutterings of discontent that it had to be abandoned. Another parliament was summoned, and out of this Oliver arbitrarily kept any man whom he did not think ought to come in. It was anything but a radical body, and after declaring against the rule of the major-generals, it offered Oliver the kingship, an offer to which the army objected, and which Oliver, therefore, refused; but even with this subservient assembly Oliver could not get along, and it finally shared the fate of its predecessor. The objection of the army to the kingship, was partly due to the presence of so many Republican zealots in its ranks; but probably the main reason for the objection was that the army, more or less consciously, realized that its own overmastering importance in the commonwealth would vanish as soon as the man it had made supreme by the sword was changed into a constitutional king.

One by one almost all of Oliver's old comrades and adherents left him, and he was driven to put his own kinsfolk into as many of the higher places, both in the State and the army, as possible; less from nepotism than from the need of having in important positions men who would do his will, without question. Eventually he had to abandon most of the ideas of political liberty which he had originally championed, and, following the path which the Long Parliament had already trod, he finally established a rigid censorship of the press.

Yet, though it must be freely admitted that in its later years the government of Cromwell was in form and substance a tyranny, it must be no less freely acknowledged that he used with wisdom and grandeur the power he had usurped. The faults he committed were the faults of the age, rather than special to himself, while his sincerity and honesty were peculiarly his own.

He fairly carried out his pledge of healing and settling, and he put through a long series of administrative reforms. In England and Wales his internal administration undoubtedly told for what was of moral and material advantage to the country; and if there was heavy taxation, at least it produced visible and tangible results, which was never the case under the Stuarts, before or after him. Yet his rule could not but produce discontent. In the first place, the Royalists were not well treated. In that age the beaten party was expected to pay heavily for its lack of success, both in purse and in body; and it was not to be expected that the victorious Puritans should show toward their defeated foes the generosity displayed by Grant and his fellow-victors in the American Civil War. In the American Revolution, the Tories were at first followed with much the same vindictiveness that the Royalists were followed after King Charles had been brought to the block. But Washington and all the leading American statesmen disapproved of this, and after the first heat of passion was over the American Royalists were allowed precisely the same civil and political rights as their neighbors. On the contrary, in England, under the Commonwealth, the Royalists were kept disfranchised, and taxation was arranged so as always to fall with crushing weight upon them, thus insuring their permanent alienation. As regards the rest of the people, while there was considerable interference with political and religious liberty, it was probably only what the times demanded, and was certainly much less than occurred in almost any other country. Episcopalians were denied the use of the Prayer-Book, and, like the Catholics, were given liberty of conscience only on condition that they should not practise their faith in public. Irritating though this was, and wrong though it was, it fell infinitely short of what had been done to Protestants, under Queen Mary, by the temporarily victorious Catholics, or to Puritans and Catholics under Queen Elizabeth, or of what was to be done to the Covenanters of Scotland, under the victorious Episcopalians; but such considerations would not have altered the discontent, even had the discontented kept them in mind. When provocation is sufficient to drive a man into revolution, it matters little in practical politics how much beyond this point it is carried. The breaking-point is reached sooner in some nations than in others; but in all strong nations persecution will cause revolt long before it takes the terrible form given it by Spaniards and Turks; and, once the war is on, the men who revolt hate any persecutor so much that there is scant room for intensification of the feeling. Moreover, instead of the Cromwellian government growing more, it grew less tolerant of Catholicism and Episcopacy as time went on.

The people at large were peculiarly irritated by what were merely the defects inevitably incident to the good features of Puritanism in that age. When faith is very strong and belief very sincere, men must possess great wisdom, broad charity, and the ability to learn by experience, or else they will certainly try to make others live up to their own standards. This would be bad enough, even were the standards absolutely right; and it is necessarily worse in practice than in theory, inasmuch as mixed with the right there is invariably an element of what is wrong or foolish. The extreme exponents and apologists of any fervent creed can always justify themselves, in the realm of pure logic, for insisting that all the world shall be made to accept and act up to their standards, and that they must necessarily strive to bring this about, if they really believe what they profess to believe. Of course, in practice, the answer is that there are hundreds of different creeds, or shades of creeds, all of which are believed in with equal devoutness by their followers, and therefore in a workaday government it is necessary to insist that none shall interfere with any other. Where people are as far advanced in practical good sense and in true religious toleration as in the United States to-day, the great majority of each creed gradually grows to accept this position as axiomatic, and the smaller minority is kept in check without effort, both by law and by public opinion.

In Cromwell's time, such law did not obtain in any land, and public opinion was not ripe for it. He was far in advance of his fellow-Englishmen. He described their attitude perfectly, and indeed the attitude of all Europe, when he remarked: "Every sect saith, Oh, give me liberty! but, given it and to spare, he will not yield it to anyone else. Liberty of conscience is a natural right, and he that would have it ought to give it.... I desire it from my heart; I have prayed for it; I have watched for the day to see union and right understanding between the Godly people—Scots, English, Jews, Gentiles, Presbyterians, Independents, Anabaptists, and all."

The whole principle of religious toleration is summed up in these brief sentences. In his higher and better moments, and far more than most men of his generation, Cromwell tried to live up to them. When Mazarin, the great French cardinal, in responding to Cromwell's call for toleration of the Vaudois, asked toleration for English Catholics, Cromwell answered, truly, that he had done all he could in face of the hostile spirit of the people, and more than had before been done in England. Of course the position of the English Catholics was beyond all comparison better than that of the Vaudois; but in such a controversy the ugly fact was that neither side would grant to others what it demanded for itself. To the most persecuted of all peoples Cromwell did render a signal service. He connived at the settlement of Jews in London, after having in vain sought to bring about their open toleration.

In Scotland, the rule of the Protector wrought unmixed good. There was no persecution and no interference with religious liberty, save in so far as the restraint of persecution and intolerance could itself be called such. Monk, and Dean, after him, as Cromwell's lieutenants, did excellent work, and even cautiously endeavored to mitigate the horrors of the persecutions for witchcraft—for these horrible manifestations of superstition were then in full force in Scotland, even more than in either old or New England.

On the whole, then, England and Scotland fared well under Oliver Cromwell—"Old Noll," as he was affectionately called by his mainstay, the army. In Ireland, the case was different. Materially, even in Ireland, the conditions greatly improved during the Protectorate, because order was rigidly preserved and law enforced; and any system which secured order and law was bound to bring about a temporary bettering of conditions when contrasted with the frightful anarchy which had preceded it. Anarchy always serves simply as the handmaiden of despotism, as those who bring it about should know. But the religious element in the Irish problem rendered it insoluble by the means then adopted for its solution. Cromwell was not responsible for introducing the methods known by his name. They were the methods then universally in use by the representatives of every victorious nationality or religion, in dealing with a beaten foe. The only difference was that Cromwell's immense energy and power enabled him to apply them with dreadful effectiveness.

In England, Cromwell stood for religious toleration, so far as he was able. Fanatics who thought themselves incarnations of the

Saviour, or prophets of a new dispensation, or who indulged in indecent or seditious conduct, or who disturbed the public peace by breaking into regular churches, of course had to be suppressed. Nowadays, most offenders of this type would be ignored, and, if not, they would simply be arrested by the police, in the course of the ordinary exercise of the police power, just as any other disturbers of the peace are arrested. In those days, however, such offenders would have been punished with death in Spain, Italy, or Austria; and, indeed, in most continental countries. In the England of Cromwell, they were merely temporarily imprisoned. The attitude of mind, both of the public generally and of the best and most religious people, toward Unitarians, Socinians, and those who would nowadays be called Free-Thinkers, was purely mediæval; and even Cromwell could only moderate the persecution to which they were subjected. But these were minor exceptions. For the majority of the people in England, there was religious liberty; and for the bulk of the minority, though there was not complete religious liberty, there was a nearer approach to it than obtained in Continental Europe.

In Ireland, on the other hand, the public exercise of the faith of the enormous majority was prohibited, and their religious teachers expelled. There is a popular belief that under Cromwell all Irishmen were expelled from three-fourths of the island, and driven into Connaught, their places being taken by English and Scotch immigrants. While exceedingly cruel, this would have been an understandable policy, and would have resulted in the substitution of one race and one creed for another race and another creed throughout the major part of the island. What was actually done, however, combined cruelty with ultimate inefficiency; it caused great immediate suffering, while perpetuating exactly the conditions against which it was supposed to provide. The Catholic landholders were, speaking generally, driven into Connaught, and the priests expelled, while the peasants, laborers, and artisans were left as they were, but of course deprived of all the leadership which could give them a lift upward. In Ulster there had been a considerable substitution of one race for the other, among the actual tillers and occupiers of the soil. Under Cromwell, the change elsewhere consisted in the bringing in of alien landlords. In other words, to the already existing antagonism of race, creed, and speech, was added the antagonism of caste. The property-holder, the landlord, the man of means, was an Englishman by race and speech, and a Protestant by faith; while the mass of the laborers roundabout him were Catholic Celts who spoke Erse. Ultra admirers of Cromwell and the Puritans have actually spoken as if this plan, provided only that it had been allowed to work long enough, would have produced a Puritan Ireland. There was never the remotest chance of its producing such an effect. The mass of the Irish, when all their native teachers were removed, did gradually tend to adopt English as their tongue, but their devotion to their own faith, and their hatred of English rule, were merely intensified; while the course of the governing race was such as absolutely to insure the land troubles which have riven Ireland up to the present day. The very unedifying intolerance of the Protestant sects toward one another was manifested as strongly in Cromwell's time as later. It must be said for him that he did not, like his successors for generations, shape English policy toward Ireland on the lines of Spain's policy toward her own colonies, and oppress the Protestant descendants of the English in Ireland only less than the native Irish themselves; but the great central fact remains that his Irish policy was one of bitter oppression, and that the abhorrence with which the Irish, to this day, speak of "the curse o' Crummle," is historically justifiable.

It is a relief to turn from the Cromwellian policy in Ireland to the Cromwellian policy in foreign affairs. England never stood higher in her relations with the outside world than she stood under Cromwell; a height all the more noteworthy because it lay between the two abysses marked by the policy of the earlier and the later Stuart kings. The French biographer of the great Turenne, du Buisson, Major of the Regiment de Verdelin, writing in the days of Charles II., when England was despised rather than hated on the Continent, spoke with a mixture of horror and fear of Cromwell, as the man who "après l'attentat le plus énorme dont on a jamais ouï parler, avoit trouvé le secret de se faire craindre, non seulement des Anglois, mais encore des Princes voisins." This was written as expressing the attitude of the power with which he was in alliance, and from it may be gathered how those felt who were opposed to him.

Cromwell's strong religious feelings and military instincts, alike bade him meddle in the policy of the Continent. The era of the great religious wars was closed. More than a century was to pass before the era of religious persecution was to cease, but the time had gone by when one Christian country would try, by force of arms, to conquer another for the purpose of stamping out its religious belief. Cromwell, however, did not see this, and he naturally chose as his special opponent the power which itself was equally blind to the fact—that is, Spain. Beyond a question, he was influenced partly by the commercial and material interests of England in the policy he pursued, but the religious motive was uppermost in his own mind, and he never could get over the feeling that it ought to be uppermost in the minds of everyone else. The very able Swedish King, Charles X., was then pursuing the fatal policy of the Swedish kings of that century, and was endeavoring to conquer territory at the expense of the Danes and North Germans, instead of establishing, to the east and southeast of the Baltic, a dominion which could hold its own against Russia. Cromwell selected the Swede as the natural enemy of Antichrist, and wished to back him in a general religious war. He was amusingly irritated with the English, because they would not feel as he did, and even more with the Dutch, Danes, and Brandenburgers for declining to let themselves be made the tools of the northern king's ambition.

The great European struggle of the day, however, was that between Spain and France, and for some time Cromwell hesitated which side to take. He has often been blamed for not striking against France, the rising power, whose then youthful king was at a later day to threaten all Europe, and only to be held in check by coalitions in which England was the chief figure. But, though France persecuted the Huguenots more or less, just as England did the Irish Catholics, she was far more advanced than Spain, which was the most bigoted and reactionary power of Europe, both in religion and in politics. The Spanish empire was still very great. Though her power on sea had gone, on land she had on the whole held her own against the French armies, and, with England as her ally, she might for the time being have remained the leading power of the Continent. This would have been a frightful calamity, and Cromwell was right in throwing the weight of his sword on the other side of the scale.

His decision enabled him to do one of the most righteous of his many righteous deeds. It was at this time that the Duke of Savoy, under ecclesiastical pressure, indulged in dreadful persecutions of the humble Protestants of the Vaudois valleys; persecutions which called forth the noblest of Milton's sonnets. Oliver interfered, with fiery indignation, on behalf of the Vaudois, threatening that if the persecutions continued he would not only bring the pressure of the English arms to bear, but would hire a great force of mercenaries among the Protestant Swiss to invade the territory of the Duke of Savoy. Largely through the influence of Mazarin he succeeded in having the wrong partially undone; and later, in the middle of the operations against the Spanish armies, he again interfered, effectively, with the Cardinal-Statesman on behalf of his obscure and helpless co-religionists in the remote mountain valleys. This action was purely disinterested; and those who are loudest in their denunciation of Cromwell would do well to remember that, if the European rulers at the end of the nineteenth century had possessed his capacity for generous indignation on behalf of the oppressed, the Armenian massacres either would never have taken place, or would have been followed by the immediate expulsion of the Turk from Europe.

Oliver's first contest with the Spaniards was carried on by sea, the great Puritan Admiral, Blake, winning renown by his victory over the forts at Santa Cruz, as he had already won renown by the way in which he crushed the forces of Tunis, and for the first time taught the Moors to respect English arms. An expedition against San Domingo by Penn and Venables failed, the English leaders being treacherous and inefficient, but it resulted in the capture of

Jamaica and the founding of English power in the West Indies. On land, as the result of the convention with France, the English fleet deprived the Spaniards in the Netherlands of assistance from the sea, while an English force of 6,000 troops, clad in the red uniform which has since become distinctive of the British army, was sent to serve under Turenne. They overthrew the flower of the Spanish infantry, and won the heartiest praise from the great French leader. The help given by Cromwell was decisive; the Spaniards were beaten and forced to make peace. By this peace France became the first power on the Continent, but a power heartily afraid of England while Cromwell lived, and obliged to yield him Dunkirk as the price of his services. The possession of Dunkirk put a complete stop to the piracy which had ravaged British commerce, and gave to Cromwell a foothold on the Continent which rendered him able to enforce from his neighbors whatever consideration the honor and interest of England demanded.

Meanwhile, the tone of his Court was a model of purity and honesty. Alone among the Courts of Europe in that age, under Cromwell no man could rise who was profligate in private life, or corrupt in public life. How he had risen socially is shown by the fact that his remaining daughters now married into the nobility. His domestic relations were exceptionally tender and beautiful, and his grief at the loss of his mother and his favorite daughter—his favorite son was already dead—was very great. His letters to and about his sons are just what such letters should be. He explains that he does not grudge them "laudable recreations nor honorable carriage in them," nor any legitimate expense, but that he does emphatically protest against "pleasure and self-satisfaction being made the business of a man's life."

The time had now come, however, when Oliver was to leave alike the family for whom he had so affectionately cared, and the nation he had loved and ruled, and go before the God to whom he ever felt himself accountable. When 1658 opened, peace and order obtained at home, and the crown had been put to England's glory abroad by the victories in Flanders and the cession of Dunkirk. There was not the slightest chance of Cromwell's hold on the nation being shaken. So far as human eye could see, his policy was sure to triumph, as long as he lived; but he was weakened by his hard and strenuous life, and the fever, by which he had been harassed during his later campaigns, came on him with renewed force. Even his giant strength had been overtaxed by the task of ruling England alone, and, as he conscientiously believed, for her highest interest. Supreme though his triumph seemed to outsiders, he himself knew that he had failed to make the effects of this triumph lasting, though he never seems to have suspected that his failure was due to his incapacity to subordinate his own imperious will so that he might work with others. He saw clearly the chaos into which his death would plunge England, and he did not wish to die; but as he grew weaker he felt that his hour was come, and surrendered himself to the inevitable.

"I would be willing to live to be further serviceable to God and His people," muttered the dying ruler, showing, as ever, his strange mixture of belief in himself and trust in the Most High; "but my work is done! Yet God will be with His people!"

September came in with a terrible storm, the like of which had rarely been known in England, and as it subsided, on September 3d, the day which had witnessed the victories of Dunbar and Worcester, the soul of the greatest man who has ruled England, since the days of the Conquest, passed quietly away.

With his death came the chaos he had foreseen, though he had not foreseen that it could be averted only by the substitution of some form of self-government by the people, for the arbitrary rule of one man—however great and good that man might be. For a few months his son, Richard, ruled as Protector in his stead, but, the Protectorate having become in effect a despotism, it was sure to slip from any but Oliver's iron grasp. Richard called a Parliament, but Parliaments had been hopelessly discredited by Oliver's method of dealing with them. The army revolted, forced the dismissal of the Parliament, and then the abdication of Richard. Richard's abler brother, Henry, who was governing Ireland as deputy, resigned also, and the Cromwells passed out of history.

For some months there was confusion worse confounded, and the whole nation turned toward Charles II., and the re-establishment of the Stuart kingship. Monk, the ablest of Cromwell's generals, a soldier who cared little for forms of civil government, who had already fought for the Stuarts against the Parliament, and who would have stood by Richard had Richard possessed the strength to stand by himself, threw his weight in favor of the exiled king, and thereby prevented the slightest chance of opposition. Charles II. returned, greeted with transports of frantic delight by seemingly almost the whole people.

The King and his followers then took revenge on the dead body of the man whose living eyes they had never dared to face. The bones of Cromwell, of his mother, and of Ireton, were disinterred and thrown into a lime-pit; and the head of the great Protector was placed on a pole over Westminster Hall, there to stand for twenty years.

The skull of the mighty crown-grasper, before whose untamable soul they had shuddered in terror, was now set on high as a target for the jeering mockery of all who sang the praises of the line of libertines and bigots to whom the English throne had been restored. For twenty-eight shameful years the Restoration lasted; years of misgovernment and persecution at home, of weakness abroad, of oppression of the weak, and obsequious servility to the strong; years when the Court of England—devoid of one spark of true greatness of any kind—was a scene of tawdry and obscene frivolity. Then, once again, the principles for which, in the last analysis, Cromwell and the Puritans stood, triumphed; the Dutch stadtholder came over the narrow seas to ascend the throne of England; and once more the current of her national life set toward political, intellectual, and religious liberty.

Cromwell and the Puritans had gone too far, and the reaction against them had been so violent that those who called William of Orange into England dared not invoke the memory of the mighty dead lest they should hurt the cause of the living. Nevertheless, the Revolution of 1688 was in reality but the carrying on of the work which had been done in the middle of the century. James II. could never have been deposed had not

Charles I. been executed. The men of the second Revolution had learned the moderation which the men of the first had lacked. They were careful not to kill the king of whom they wished to rid themselves; for though, by every principle of equity, a tyrant who has goaded his people into Revolution—like the leader of an unjustifiable rebellion—should suffer the fate which he has brought on so many others, yet, as a matter of fact, it is often unwise to treat him as he deserves, because he has become a symbol to his followers, each of whom identifies himself with the man whose cause he has been supporting, and in whose name he has been fighting, and resents, with passionate indignation, any punishment visited upon his chief as a wrong in which he personally shares. The men of 1688 were, as a whole, actuated by far less lofty motives than the men of 1648; but they possessed the inestimable advantages of common-sense, of moderation, of readiness to accept compromises. They made no attempt to realize the reign of the saints upon earth; and therefore they were able to work a permanent betterment in mundane affairs, and to avoid provoking a violent reaction. William, both by position and by temper, was far better fitted than great Oliver to submit to interference with his plans, to get on with representative bodies of freemen, and to make the best he could out of each situation as it arose, instead of indignantly setting his own will above law and above the will of the majority, because for the moment the result might be better for himself and the nation. Speaker Reed once said, that "in the long run, the average sense of the many is better for the many than the best sense of any one man;" and this is undoubtedly true of all people sufficiently high in the scale to be fit for self-government.

Oliver surely strove to live up to his lights as he saw them. He never acted in levity, or from mere motives of personal aggrandizement, and he saw, with sad, piercing eyes, the dangers that rolled around the path he had chosen. He acted as he did because he conscientiously felt that only thus could he meet the needs of the nation. He said to the second Protectorate Parliament: "I am a man standing in the place I am in; which place I undertook, not so much out of hope of doing any good, as out of a desire to prevent mischief and evil—which I did see was imminent on the nation (for we were running along into confusion and disorder, and would have necessarily run into blood)."

After Charles II. succeeded to the throne, the bones of Cromwell were disinterred and his head exposed upon a pole over Westminster Hall, almost on the identical spot where the Cromwell statue, shown in the right of the drawing, has just been erected.

We are often told that the best of all possible governments would be a benevolent despotism. Oliver's failure is a sufficient commentary upon this dictum of the parlor doctrinaires. There never has been, and probably never will be, another despotism where the despot so sincerely strove to do, for a people capable of some measure of freedom, better than they themselves would have done with that freedom. The truth is, that a strong nation can only be saved by itself, and not by a strong man, though it can be greatly aided and guided by a strong man. A weak nation may be doomed anyhow, or it may find its sole refuge in a despot; a nation struggling out of darkness may be able to take its first steps only by the help of a master hand, as was true of Russia, under Peter the Great; and if a nation, whether free or unfree, loses the capacity for self-government, loses the spirit of sobriety and of orderly liberty, then it has no cause to complain of tyranny; but a really great people, a people really capable of freedom and of doing mighty deeds in the world, must work out its own destiny, and must find men who will be its leaders—not its masters. Cromwell could, in all probability, have been such a leader at the end as he was during his early years of public life; and when he permitted himself to fall from the position of a leader among free men, to that of a master over men for whose welfare he sincerely strove, but in whose freedom he did not believe, he marred the great work he had done. Nevertheless, it was a very great work. There are dark blots on his career—especially his Irish policy—but on the whole he was a mighty force for good and against evil, and the good that he did, though buried for the moment with his bones, rose again and has lived for ever since, while the evil has long withered, or is now withering. The English-speaking peoples are free, and for good or for ill hold their destinies in their own hands.

The effect of the attitude which not only the Puritans, but all other Englishmen of every creed, assumed toward Ireland from the days of Queen Mary to the days of King George the Fourth, was such as to steep the island in centuries of misery, and to leave in her people a bitter and enduring hatred against England. Yet this attitude has produced one result of the most unforeseen kind. Had the Irish remained a Celtic nation, separate in speech and government from Great Britain, they could have had no share in the expansion of the English race, or at least could have played only a very subordinate part. As it is, in the great English-speaking commonwealths that have grown up in North America and Australasia, the descendants of the Irish now stand on an exact equality with those of the Scotch and English, and furnish their full proportion of leadership in the government of the communities; while in all these English-speaking countries the Catholic Church has become one of the leading churches and has had its course of development determined by the fact that the controlling force within it has been Irish. The English Protestants failed to impress their creed upon Ireland, but they did impress their language, and did bring Ireland under their own government The strange outcome has been that the creed they hated now flourishes side by side, on equal terms, with the creeds they professed, in the distant continents held in common by their children and by the children of those against whom they warred. In these new continents all, Catholics and Protestants alike, are wedded to the principles of political liberty for which the Puritans fought, and have grown to extend to all creeds the principles of religious liberty in which only the best and most advanced Puritans believed. Let us most earnestly hope that, while avoiding the Puritan fanaticism and intolerance, the Puritan lack of charity and narrowness, we may not lose the Puritan loftiness of soul and stern energy in striving for the right, than which no nation could ever have more precious heritages.

With Oliver's death his memory passed under a cloud, through which his greatness was to be but dimly seen until generations of men had lived and died. He left many descendants, and there are now in England, and also in America, and possibly Australia, very many men and women, in all ranks of life, who have his blood in their veins—though in the direct line his name has died out. Even during the present century, when among the English upper classes it was still customary to speak of him with horror, his very descendants in certain families felt keen shame for the deeds of their great forefather. With a childishness in no way above that of a Congo savage, it was actually the fashion in some of these families to make the children do penance on the anniversary of the death of Charles II., as a kind of atonement for the deeds of Cromwell. The grotesque nature of this performance is added to by the fact that in that very society a peculiarly high place of honor was accorded to the titled descendants of Charles II. and his mistresses. One hardly knows whether to be most amused or indignant at such fantastic incapacity to appreciate what was really noble and what really ignoble. The men among whom such false conventions obtained could not be expected to see in its true proportions the form of mighty Oliver, looming ever larger across the intervening centuries. Sooner or later, justice will be done him; sooner or later, he will be recognized, not only as one of the greatest of all Englishmen, and by far the greatest ruler of England itself, but as a man who, in times that tried men's souls, dealt with vast questions and solved tremendous problems; a man who erred, who was guilty of many shortcomings, but who strove mightily toward the light as it was given him to see the light; a man who had the welfare of his countrymen and the greatness of his country very close to his heart, and who sought to make the great laws of righteousness living forces in the government of the world.

Printed in Great Britain
by Amazon

22425196R00088